DOBEREINER ON GOLF... AND MORE

DOBEREINER ON GOLF

... and more

PETER DOBEREINER

Edited by Robert Green
and Ruth Dobereiner

Foreword by Severiano Ballesteros

Illustrated by Brian Bagnall

AURUM PRESS

First published in Great Britain 1998 by
Aurum Press Ltd, 25 Bedford Avenue, London WC1B 3AT

A catalogue record for this book is available from the British Library.

ISBN 1 85410 589 2

Design by Roger Lightfoot

Typeset in 10.5/13 Palatino by York House Typographic Ltd, London
Printed and bound in Great Britain by MPG Books, Bodmin

Contents

Foreword

By SEVERIANO BALLESTEROS
Three times Open champion, twice Masters champion and captain of the 1997 European Ryder Cup team

I suppose it was at the 1976 Open Championship at Royal Birkdale that I first came to the attention of the world's golfing press. Peter Dobereiner was among them. I was not then aware of Peter, but over the years I came to enjoy the quality of his work and to appreciate who he was – a champion among golf writers.

Sometimes Peter would be critical about me, as well as about other players, but always it was either in a humorous way or else his comments would be deserved. The fact was that he loved the game of golf, and he knew a great deal about it. I am delighted to note that in this collection of his work there are two pieces about me. I think that many of the articles in this book help to prove that Peter knew what he was talking about. Not only was he capable of making you laugh, many of the things he predicted came to happen.

Peter was a great supporter of mine, as much as I was a fan of his. When he was ill in the summer of 1996, we exchanged letters, and I will always treasure the kind remarks he made to me. And although I knew he was not well, it was still a huge shock to learn that he had died. The world of golf suddenly became a poorer place. He was a great man – kind, knowledgeable, clever and funny.

Peter would loved to have been at Valderrama in September 1997 to see Europe retain the Ryder Cup. He adored the Ryder Cup, and he was a great friend of Valderrama and of golf in Spain. That week was one of the highlights of my career, and it would have been wonderful if Peter could have been there to share it. But maybe, up there somewhere, he was watching us.

I hope you enjoy this book. I am very sure you will.

Regards.

My father

Golf writers are a strange breed and I'm not sure they ought to be allowed to have children. Their minds, let's face it, are on other things. In the few months of the year that my father was at home, he could never be trusted to collect any of us kids from school for fear that he would arrive back with some completely unknown infant. Giving the speech at my wedding he was so anxious to get the name of the groom right that he proceeded to tell ribald stories about the early years of the wrong daughter. Such was his reputation for eccentricity, the lapse was barely noticed, not even by my mother.

Readers of this book, however, will be more concerned with his deliberations on golf than his devoted although sometimes misguided attempts at fatherhood. To his many colleagues and fans in the world of golf he may have been a legend (as indeed I later found out he was). To us kids, though, he was a father first, a constant source of amusement, love, support, entertainment, inspiration and mirth. Particularly mirth. When he died, it felt as if a nation were intruding on our personal grief.

This anthology acknowledges not only the forty years or so of writing about the sport he loved but couldn't really play, but also the many other talents he had: script-writing (he was one of the original team of writers for the BBC's award-winning *That Was the Week, That Was*), speech-writing, anecdote telling and generally commenting on life as deciphered from the bottom of a bottle of good claret.

He once said that he had children the way other people have

mice. Despite his ambition to produce the next Masters Champion, all four rodents, having witnessed what life in the golfing profession had done for their father, turned their talents to more respectable occupations. And the money's not bad for topless dancers these days.

He is missed beyond measure, but qualities such as his live on, in the foibles, the fun and the family that always held him as their personal hero.

This one's for you, Pop.

RUTH DOBEREINER

Introduction

I first met Peter Dobereiner at one of the early Bob Hope Classic tournaments at Moor Park, the week Peter enjoyed pointing out – how shall we say this? – one or two discrepancies in the way the event was run. James Garner, one of the celebrity guests on view that week, read the offending article in the *Observer* and went around demanding to know who the hell this 'Doberman' was. Being cast as one of the more vicious of household pets was rather out of kilter with the character most people knew, but not entirely inappropriate. Peter could be dogged in the pursuit of his profession. And he could write.

One of the best Dobereiner anecdotes makes both points nicely. In the days of yore, reporting golf tournaments from the continent was given an extra *frisson* of the exotic by the invariable chaos of the telephone systems. One Saturday afternoon in Madrid, Peter's attempts to get through to his newspaper were rewarded some ninety minutes later than he had hoped. He was eventually directed by the press officer to a dingy cubicle, where he found himself miraculously connected to a copy-taker in London. Relieved, Peter began to dictate his 800-word story.

About halfway through this process, and mightily thankful the line had not yet gone dead on him, Peter was interrupted mid-flow by the strong cockney accent on the other end.

'Hey, guv, don't you think that word's a bit strong?'

'What do you mean?'

'I mean "mellifluous".'

'I'm perfectly sure that readers of the *Observer* know what mellifluous means.'

'I dare say, mate, but this isn't the *Observer*. It's the *People*.'

The awful truth dawned that the press officer had directed him to the wrong phone. But Dobereiner's apologies, tinged with dismay at having to suffer the whole rigmarole again, were broken by the voice cheerily saying, 'It doesn't matter. This is better than the crap I normally get here. You finish it off and I'll send it on to your paper.'

By the time I met Peter that first time at the Hope, he was unquestionably the doyen of British golf writers. From his behaviour, you would never have known it. He was a big man in every sense – in his personality, his physique, his intellect and his heart. The fact that I was a tyro was irrelevant. He was charming and helpful. He treated everyone the same.

In latter years I was to discover that he was the perfect writer to have the pleasure of editing – his copy was terrific to read, technically accomplished and punctual. If you needed help in getting out of hole, were desperate for the conjuring up of a fast thousand words of wit, wisdom or both, Peter was your man. And he believed in letting editors edit. No airs and graces with him – if his piece needed cutting and amending in some way, he trusted you to do it. Of course, it hardly ever did. He could write to length, too.

In a way, it is hard to assess the respect in which he was held by his peers. In many respects, he had no peers. Rather, he was the successor to Bernard Darwin and Henry Longhurst as *the* golf writer of his generation. Dai Davies, who has admirably stepped into Peter's shoes as golf correspondent at both the *Guardian* and the *Observer*, put it well when he wrote of Peter: 'He was, perhaps, the most rounded man, the most civilized man, even the most erudite man to embrace and grace a golfing press tent.'

Peter read law at Oxford and served as a Fleet Air Arm pilot in World War II. Before becoming a golf writer, he worked for several years in Fleet Street and was a script-writer for *That*

Was The Week, That Was. (Although some of this anthology has appeared between hard covers before, the marvellous TW3 material herein has not.) In addition to writing for the *Observer* for twenty-five years, and later for the *Guardian*, he wrote what he called 'a yard of books', later in life collaborated with Sir Henry Cotton on the design of the Alto Club in Portugal – he was a member of the American Society of Golf Course Architects – and drank red wine with an infectious enthusiasm, all the while vehemently insisting: 'I am a consumer, not a connoisseur.' White wine was summarily dismissed as battery acid.

Jerry Tarde, the editor of *Golf Digest*, who also had the joy of working with Peter for many years, captured the quality of his work, the Dobereiner legacy, in the eulogy he delivered at Peter's funeral.

> He taught us to laugh, to laugh at our golf, especially to laugh at ourselves. And when he went, he didn't take the laughter with him. How lucky we are that he left us with his written words ... He's there in every line of them. Making us stop and think, with smiles on our faces.

We hope that this book does that for you.

I last saw Peter two days before he died, on August 2, 1996. Although in discomfort and some pain, he remained as amusing and perceptive, as courteous and charming, as he always was – and just as he had been all those years ago at Moor Park.

ROBERT GREEN

ONE: PLAYERS AND PEOPLE

The pirate from Spain.

A letter to Nick Faldo

Dear Nick Faldo,

As a striker of a golf ball you are beginning to be mentioned in the same breath as Ben Hogan, even by some people who actually saw Ben Hogan strike golf balls. I endorse that judgment, in terms of the long game. Hogan had his moments on the greens, but overall you are a much, much better putter than he was and I hope that soon people will start to mention your putting in the same breath as Ben Crenshaw's.

Your intention is to win all four major championships every year until at least the end of the century, a worthy ambition that by my reckoning would give you a total of 40, double the tally of Jack Nicklaus. You happen to have achieved your current dominance in an era of golfing plonkers and I cannot see anyone on the horizon with the remotest chance of foiling your intentions. I wish you well in your noble crusade.

You have also said that you want to help bring golf to the people and make it available to youngsters. As everyone knows, a boy who wants to take up the game is currently about as popular on the greens as a plague of leather-jacketed motorcyclists. Here again you have my good wishes in your campaign to provide golf, and golf instruction, at a cost that everyone can afford.

But there is a serious conflict between your twin ambitions. As you will recognize, to achieve your playing ambitions you will have to refine your game to the point where you never miss a fairway, hit every approach shot close to the flagstick and then sink every putt. You are a perfectionist and you might indeed come close to that elusive ideal.

If so, you would achieve your playing ambitions, but at what cost? Everyone else would be forced to work as hard as you, and along similarly enlightened lines, and they would approach perfection. Pro golf would become unwatchable and would die.

Don't worry, you reply, perfection is impossible in golf because the luck of the bounce will always be there. I am not so sure, the way golf course architecture and maintenance is going. But there is another point. As the greatest player in the world, every golfer is going to copy your example. What will that do to the game?

Historically, golf has enjoyed unprecedented periods of expansion when the role model has been an erratic player. Walter Hagen never knew where his ball was going and he had to invent six or seven new shots every time he played just to get his ball back into play. Arnold Palmer was the same, with the added element of excitement that at any moment his trousers might fall down. Tom Watson never hit more than three fairways in one round, and, by the standards of the instruction books, Lee Trevino hadn't the faintest idea of how to swing a club. Among them they recruited millions of new golfers and spectators.

What was Ben Hogan's legacy to golf? He is remembered mainly for a few excruciatingly rude remarks. What did Jack Nicklaus do for golf? Everybody copied his deliberate manner of play and gave us the six-hour round. The game was dying on its feet until Seve Ballesteros came along in the nick of time with his slam-bang style. Everyone could relate to him because we can all fire it into the woods.

No, I am not suggesting that you should deliberately develop a flaw in your swing to make the golf more exciting. All I am asking is that you be aware of your heavy responsibilities to the overall good of the game. I was rather hoping on the final day at the British Open at St Andrews, when you had the championship in your pocket and had prevailed over Mr Excitement himself, Greg Norman, the day before, that you would deliberately hit into a few bunkers. After all, you must have known that the only possible threat would slip up because his main purpose in being on the course was to advertise vulgar taste in golfwear. You could have popped one onto the road at the seventeenth and still won with strokes to spare.

My advice is that you perfect your recovery shots. Then, once you have the situation well under control, you can enjoy yourself by devising private challenges. 'What if I were to pull-hook a drive onto that tiny island in the middle of the lake and then blast a 3-wood over the trees onto the green?' That sort of thing. That would do a world of good both for you and for golf. After all, nobody loves a machine and nobody would want to take up a game that a machine can play better than a human.

This was written shortly after Nick Faldo had won the 1990 Open Championship at St Andrews with a major-championship record low total of 18 under par (since equalled by Tiger Woods at the 1997 Masters). It was Faldo's fourth major in all, and his second of the season – at Augusta in April he had become only the second man to retain the Masters title. Faldo has since won two more majors, the 1992 Open and the 1996 Masters.

(GOLF DIGEST 1990)

Ben Hogan – detached, one bedroom

Acurious foible of human nature makes us want our sporting heroes to be warm, outgoing personalities with a ready wit and a ready grin, generous to a fault, loyal, trusty and kind to animals and little children. It is understandable, up to a point. If we have chosen them to represent us as our champions at sport, we get a stronger vicarious charge out of their triumphs if they are like us.

But nice guys come in second.

If I pick someone to live out my sporting fantasies, I want a man who will win and win and win. Experience shows that this man has to be a cold-eyed gunfighter with iced water in his veins, a ruthless killer, a single-minded, dedicated loner who doesn't give a damn about anyone or anything else.

In short, I want Ben Hogan.

Nobody wanted Hogan in the early years of his career before World War II. There wasn't much in the way of prize money and Hogan didn't even win his share of the pittance.

It was all too easy to see why. He gripped his clubs with the left palm facing down and the right palm facing up so he was always fighting, and never overcoming, a vicious hook. The price he paid for his golfing sins was that he was forced to live mostly on candy bars and oranges.

After the war, things picked up slightly. He had his moments but nobody, except Hogan himself, saw him in terms of a future champion. We could not see past his boyhood friend who had beaten him in the caddie championship at Fort Worth, and had been burying him ever since with a streak of sustained virtuosity, the like of which we shall never see again.

Then Byron Nelson checked and crosschecked the figures in his little notebook, confirmed he had enough to buy his ranch and a herd of Texas longhorns and announced his retirement.

It was 1946 and Hogan made his move. He won twelve tournaments, including the PGA Championship at Portland (Oregon) Golf Club, in which the lightest man in the field at 135 pounds had a convincing 6-&-4 victory over the heaviest, the 220-pound Ed (Porky) Oliver.

Hogan's first major has branded 1946 as a watershed year in the eyes of many golf historians. It was fifty years ago, and naturally at this year's PGA we should give the feat a moment of silence. But, I must add, it requires a tortured logic to place too much importance on Hogan's victory because the PGA was not a major in 1946. As with the Masters, those formative years and their winners became canonized retrospectively.

If you want a watershed year you cannot do better than 1953, when Hogan played a limited schedule of six events because of the painful and debilitating effects of the road accident that nearly killed him in 1949. He won five of them, including the little slam of Masters, US Open and British Open. Conflicting dates meant he could not enter the PGA.

Experienced observers at Augusta reckoned that Hogan's play that week surely represented the finest four successive rounds of tournament golf in history. Hogan confirmed that it was the best he had ever played for 72 holes.

Hogan got better and better, and the time is approaching when we must ponder all the imponderables and decide who was the greatest golfer of all time.

Jack Nicklaus takes the title of the most successful without a serious challenge. Walter Hagen enslaved the nation, and beyond, with his dashing golf and character. He must be on the short list. I feel strongly that the title of greatest golfer must be judged both on play and on personality, otherwise Iron

Byron, the USGA's mechanical golfer, would be a candidate. Hagen's golf had serious deficiencies but he scores highly on personality.

For consistently high marks right across all the subdivisions of the two categories, I give the palm to Bobby Jones.

As for Hogan, he drops a few points in the putting department, but for my money he scores a perfect 100 per cent with every other club in the bag. I have never seen, or heard, such quality and consistency of shotmaking. In his last championship round at Baltusrol in 1967, he was applauded every step of the way, like a sonic Mexican wave.

When he got to the greens, grown men could not bear to watch his tormenting yips. They turned away and tears were shed. Some of them were mine.

By the time he retired, he had won the heart of the nation because everyone loves a battler and Ben Hogan has more guts than any golfer I know.

So did he finally scrape up enough points in the personality category to tip the balance in his favour? It is a desperately close call on my scorecard, but I had to place him a point behind Jones because of something he did when he built his ten-room retirement home.

He put in only one bedroom.

Ben Hogan died in July 1997. This piece was published in July 1996, less than a month before Peter died.

(GOLF DIGEST 1996)

Vardon dodges the Titanic and history

The enormous (11" × 13½"), weighty (five pounds) and beautifully illustrated book, *Golf: The Greatest Game*, produced to celebrate the centenary of the United States Golf Association, is curiously reticent about a man whose influence on the development of golf in America was probably as potent as that of any other individual.

Harry Vardon is dismissed in two brief references, once to record the bare fact of a visit to promote a golf ball, and second in a piece about notable golfing collapses, in a story regarding his failure to win the 1920 US Open, when he dropped a stroke to par on each of the last seven holes. There is no mention of the facts that Vardon was fifty years old, had been required to play 99 holes of golf in three days, was suffering from an uncontrollable twitch in his right arm as a legacy of the disease which nearly killed him, or of the storm which sprang up at that time. O. B. Keeler, a man well versed in the sporting graces, as befitted the biographer of Bobby Jones, wrote of that 'collapse': 'Fate and nothing else beat Harry Vardon that day'.

After two false dawns, golf's sun finally rose over the United States at the turn of the century and it would have been literally impossible at that time to find a more suitable evangelist to spread the gospel of the game than Vardon. He was, after all, the only man who knew the truth of it.

He had reinvented both the style and the substance of golf. He was born on Jersey into a world which knew only the St Andrews swing: feet widely planted, two-handed grip on a club like a bludgeon and a long, flat, sweeping swing around the body designed to produce a low, boring shot into the prevailing gales of coastal Scotland.

Vardon's first appointment, after teaching himself to play as a barefoot seven-year-old hitting a clay marble with a home-made club, was as greenkeeper-professional at a 9-hole course on a nobleman's private estate in Yorkshire. Since it was used only by house guests at infrequent intervals, Vardon had plenty of time to experiment. He felt there had to be a better way to play golf, and he soon realized the advantages of hitting the ball high.

From that starting point, he developed an upright style, using lighter and more manageable clubs. This new technique permitted him to redefine the role of the longer clubs as instruments of accuracy for playing to the flagstick rather than their traditional duty of merely propelling the ball forwards to consume distance. In all essentials he created the modern swing, slightly adapted later to accommodate steel shafts and the rubber ball.

Today, he is widely credited with the invention of the Vardon grip, although this is the one element in his technique which he did not invent. A Scottish amateur, Johnny Laidlay, pioneered the overlapping grip and Vardon adopted it and, inevitably, popularized its use.

When Vardon made the first of his promotional trips to the United States, playing exhibition matches all round the country, the huge and enthusiastic crowds had the perfect role model on which to base their play. So, too, did the handful of professionals, mostly Scottish immigrants, who saw him play in, and win, the 1900 US Open.

A planned visit in 1912 had to be postponed because of Vardon's poor health. That was bad luck, you might think. But not really. After all, his passage had been booked on the maiden voyage of a liner named *Titanic*.

He made it safely the following year and had another immensely successful tour of exhibition matches. By now, he had won the Open Championship five times (eventually he made it a record six victories), and his reputation among American golf enthusiasts was, understandably enough from their experiences of him, as the invincible man.

The impact of his defeat – and Ted Ray's as well – in a playoff for the US Open at Brookline in 1913 by a young, local amateur called Francis Ouimet was accordingly seismic. This was David and Goliath in modern dress, and that sensational victory gave American golf the impetus which was to propel it into world dominance of the game. The reference to modern dress was no less than the truth, because it was Vardon who first played golf in knickerbockers and a tailored Norfolk jacket, and thus set the fashion for golfing dress which was to endure for half a century.

The fact that Harry Vardon lost the 1920 US Open, which he might well have won, is but a blip on the chart of golfing history. As I have said, he won that championship in 1900, nearly won it in 1913 and probably should have won it seven years later. If Vardon had played in the US Open every year, rather than just occasionally, as circumstances suited him, he would surely have won it frequently. But then, like that ill-proportioned book of the USGA, Vardon's record was enormously impressive.

(GOLF WORLD 1994)

The pirate from Spain

Golf instruction books can be immensely valuable to the novice. Used properly, as I am wont to advise, a book is all you need to become a champion. What you do is balance it on top of your head and then swing a club as hard as you can. Once you have mastered the art of taking a full, vicious swing without dislodging the book, you can play golf. If you should succumb to the temptation of reading it, then all is lost. It might easily take you twenty years to rinse those damaging thoughts out of your mind.

Severiano Ballesteros was immensely lucky when he started playing golf. There wasn't a golf instruction book within miles of his home in northern Spain. True, he was in some jeopardy from his elder brother Manuel, who was a tournament pro, but some native instinct saved Seve from seeking advice or listening to any hints which were volunteered in his direction. The youngster learned how to hit the ball by subconsciously absorbing the example of good players and translating these images into violent action on a trial-and-error basis.

Ballesteros also had a very good appreciation of the value of a peseta, both figuratively and literally. He used to spend hours chipping those Spanish coins into a hole, thereby acquiring an uninhibited swing and a deft touch for the delicate, stroke-saving shots. With these two assets, he has been chipping pesetas into his own pocket by the sackful ever since, winning a dozen tournaments on five continents before reaching the age of twenty-two.

It would be a gross oversimplification to ascribe Ballesteros's success to his ability as a striker alone. That is probably the lesser part of his talent. What sets him apart, in a way we have not seen since Arnold Palmer took professional golf into his massive hands and moulded it into a major spectator sport, is his buccaneering attitude.

Ballesteros is in the tradition of the pirates who sailed the Spanish Main. His instinctive impulse is to pile on all sail and run out the guns. 'I play for an eagle or a seven,' he says, and his willingness to pay the price for his swashbuckling tactics is one of his main strengths. He is out for rich plunder, and accepts risks which Jack Nicklaus would never contemplate.

As Ballesteros returns for another raid on America this spring [1979], how appropriate is it to mention his name in the same breath as that of Nicklaus? Is the handsome young Spaniard a worthy challenger for the title of world's greatest golfer?

As for the long term, I have reservations about Ballesteros's ability to approach Nicklaus's record, unless he can adjust his motives. Money is his inspiration. He refused to play for Spain in the World Cup (although he had won the contest the previous two years with different partners) because there was not enough money in it. He declined the chance to play full-time on the US Tour because there was more money, in the form of guarantees, bribes and appearance fees, on the other world circuits.

Presumably the time will come – and soon at his present rate of acquisition – when his appetite for lucre is sated. That will be the critical moment. Tony Jacklin lost his inner drive as soon as he had achieved his material objectives, and the same could happen to Ballesteros. But if the Spaniard could acquire a fresh motivation, and aspire to smash all the records for the sake of the achievement and not for any thought of reward, then I would not care to put a limit on his potential.

For the moment, we must be content to relish the sight of the most exciting golfer of his generation. He does not know the meaning of playing the percentages; he scorns dangers and once announced, 'The rough is my friend.' On the tee his one idea is to smash the ball straight at the flag; if the green is out of range, even for his inordinate length, he smashes one at the flag anyway.

Often enough, some natural feature such as a mountain, a forest or a lake intervenes. Ballesteros then seeks to blast his way forwards. In four years as a touring pro, he must have made more birdies and eagles without touching a fairway than any other player in history. He has his accurate days, but his scores on such occasions are not necessarily better than when he is in a wild mood, because his chipping and pitching are uncanny. I have seen him play shots which three hundred years ago would have condemned him to death by burning for sorcery.

He is still at some risk from fire, because his golfing style and his punishing programme must put him at risk of burning himself out. He has already damaged his back through excessive practice. He is certainly destined to join the US Tour before long, but I would advise connoisseurs to catch him on one of his limited appearances this year. It is possible there will not be too many opportunities in the future, and Ballesteros in full flight is an experience which should not be missed.

This was published in May 1979, around a year after Seve had won his first US Tour event. In fact, it would only be two months before he would win his first major championship, the Open at Royal Lytham. Within a year, he would be Masters champion.

(GOLF DIGEST 1979)

Will Seve bounce back?

Y ou either love him or you hate him. Some people do both, loving him one minute and hating him the next. Others manage to love and hate him at the same time, loving his play and his spirit while simultaneously hating his petulance at a failed putt. It is a rare person in golf who is indifferent to Severiano Ballesteros, because he is a difficult man to ignore.

At this time of year, around the Masters, the emotions generated by Ballesteros intensify, since his length and short-game genius have made him an Augusta National specialist. He has often said that it is his favourite course and, by extension, his favourite tournament. He is a repeat winner of a championship that has the best record among golf's four classics of rewarding the best players. And yet, from 1985 to 1987, Ballesteros has rather lost his way at Augusta.

Take 1985. Historically, Ballesteros could always put the whammies on Bernhard Langer. Not that year. Playing together in the final round, Langer won and Seve settled for a second-place tie.

Take 1986. Again he was right in contention until the sixty-ninth hole, where he hit a rank bad shot, catching his 4-iron so fat the ball never looked like it might make it across the pond in front of the fifteenth green.

Take 1987. By his standards, he should have had that one wrapped up, but had to go into a three-way playoff. And he was the first to falter.

A number of theories have been advanced to explain Ballesteros's decline into the status of the world's second-best golfer.

His single-minded pursuit of major championships was side-tracked by his feud with the PGA Tour's Policy Board over what he perceived to be discrimination against foreign players. The death of his father in 1986 threw him for a loop.

In Britain's popular press, whose salacious obsession with secrets of the boudoir totally eclipses any notional interest in sport, Ballesteros is presented as the victim of unrequited love. Romeo Ballesteros, son of a poor dirt farmer from the wrong side of the tracks, sighs beneath the balcony of Juliet (Carmen Botín, actually, daughter of the highborn and wealthy president of the Bank of Santander, near Seve's hometown of Pedrẽna).

'See, how she leans her cheek upon her hand! O, that I were a glove upon that hand, that I might touch that cheek!'

Juliet demonstrates that her expensive education at Cheltenham Ladies' College in England and Brown University in Rhode Island has not been wasted by responding, 'O Romeo, Romeo! Wherefore art thou, Romeo?'

The plot now thickens. In his office at the bank, father Botín studies the statement of Romeo's account. Each figure is followed by a seemingly endless row of zeroes, like the wheels of freight trains rolling across La Mancha bearing treasures to his vaults. An eminently suitable son-in-law, he concludes.

But mother Botín, the blue blood of the Capulets rising in her gorge, has a proper scorn for money, especially new money. You can, she asserts with vigour, take the boy out of the caddie shack, but you can't take the caddie shack out of the boy. I will never permit the most fragrant flower of the Capulets to be united with a Montague.

Shakespearean scholars will realize that the current state of play is roughly the end of Act II. It is possible that there resides some vestige of validity in these theories, although it would be a highly selective form of distraction that permitted Ballesteros to win fourteen tournaments in three years but thwarted him in the Masters. It is possible there will yet be a happy dénouement to this drama. Seve expects to marry Carmen this summer. Of course, he has been expecting to marry her for a couple of years now. So it is difficult to be certain.

Ballesteros has the perverse idea that his private life is, well, private. He does not hold conversations; he grants audiences. Any question deeper than 'What club did you hit?' is parried with a disarming smile and a facetious quip. For the rest, he issues declarations with all the authority of a secular pope.

'You think I should win every time I play?' [*No I don't, but let it pass.*] 'You don't know how difficult it is to win a championship.' [*Yes I do, but no matter.*] 'There are a lot of very good players.' [*Really? The very idea!*] 'Sometimes the putts do not drop for you.' [*As a matter of fact, I had observed that phenomenon.*] 'You can't imagine the pressure.' [*I can, I can.*] 'Golf is a funny game.' [*So I've heard.*]

On such occasions, the only thing to do is keep your thoughts to yourself, retreat backward from the presence, bowing as you go and count on your own reserves of observation.

So wherefore art thou, Severiano? My theory, for what it is worth, is that everything in Ballesteros's life admits of only one explanation: he is the subject of demonic possession. It is, after all, a common enough condition with champions. Gary Player's demon was his size; he was driven to prove that he could beat anyone, no matter how big and strong that person might be. Jack Nicklaus's demon was glory, and what a partnership those two made. Since there is honour in defeat no less than victory, the demon made Nicklaus not only the greatest winner in golf but also the game's most gracious loser.

Ballesteros's demon is justice. Thirty years ago Spain was still a feudal society with a sharp demarcation between the haves and the have-nots or, possibly more accurately, the somebodies and the nobodies. Ballesteros was born with a bellyful of resentment, and his determination to beat the system made him a great player.

On the PGA European Tour, his resentment boiled at the practice of paying inducements to imported stars to give tournaments prestige. His only redress was to make himself an even bigger star than the imports, hence his relish at knocking over big-name American players. He said that he liked beating Americans because they were the best players in the world, but there was more to it than that, much more. He was determined to get the same treatment as the visitors.

When he demanded appearance money, having achieved star status on his own account, he was refused, so he took himself into exile rather than suffer the injustice. He was branded a money-grubber, but cash was always an irrelevance to Ballesteros; it was the principle of equality that fired him.

His motives were similarly misconstrued in his battles with the US PGA Tour. He was hurt that his claim to be allowed to play in Europe whenever he wanted was not conceded immediately. It was ludicrous, he argued, that he could not play his home tour without releases. Telling him he could play in Spain was sheer discrimination because Spain did not have a tour. Europe was his home tour. His crusading zeal kept him simmering long enough to win a couple of green coats, but now he has got his own way or, as he would put it, justice has finally prevailed.

That is why I hope there is some substance in all that Romeo and Juliet stuff. As a crusader without a cause, Ballesteros is just another very good professional golfer. He only achieves greatness when superheated steam is bursting from his ears.

Fanaticism is a young man's game, and we all mellow with age. But if Ballesteros can get himself genuinely furious about something, then it will be the others who are playing for second place.

Ten years on: Ballesteros did not win the 1988 Masters (Sandy Lyle did), but within three months of this piece being published, he had won a third Open Championship – his second at Lytham – and soon after he did marry Carmen. They now have three children.

(GOLF DIGEST 1988)

Will Greg Norman reach superstardom?

According to the statistics of foreign prejudice, the average Australian is a potbellied drunk with bad teeth. According to the view that Australians hold of themselves, the average Australian is seven feet tall, stomach hard and flat as a spade, built like a brick outhouse with muscles abulge, teeth dazzling white grain against mahogany complexion and clipped, flaxen hair. Furthermore, he is a two-fisted, spit-in-your-eye, down-to-earth cove with none of our effete English intellectual pretensions, and the Sheila has not been born who can resist his sexual magnetism for more than seven seconds.

The mythology of this Australian stereotype is sustained by a tiny fraction of the population, of which Greg Norman is a Class A member. Norman is an Aussie's ideal of an ideal Aussie: Six-foot-one, hair the colour of whipped cream and shoulders so wide that he has to edge sideways through the average doorway.

He is deeply religious, which in Australian terms means that he is a sports freak. As a boy growing up near Moreton Bay on the eastern coast of Australia, he played them all: tennis, cricket, soccer, rugby and that curious amalgamation of the two football games plus a liberal seasoning of kung fu, Australian Rules. He also boxed and swam and surfed, and it was a reluctant sixteen-year-old who was pressed into service to caddie for his 3-handicap mother in a competition. He thought golf a sissy game and it was only curiosity after the round that prompted him to try a few shots for himself on the range. He nailed one shot and that is all it takes.

In less than two years, he was down to scratch and facing a quandary. His ambition was to be a fighter pilot, a properly macho occupation, and he had passed his examinations for flying training. His father went with him for the enrolment formalities into the Royal Australian Air Force. A squadron leader had the enlistment papers prepared and Norman had his hand poised when he tossed down the pen and announced, 'No, I am going to be a pro golfer.' For better or worse, the choice was made and he became an assistant, winning his fifth event as a pro (better) and then blowing sky-high when he was paired with his idol, Jack Nicklaus, in the Australian Open (worse).

On balance, it was a highly promising start to his career, and it was at this time he established the origins of his nickname, The Great White Shark. Like Nicklaus, he relaxed from golf by deep-sea fishing, and there are few better waters than off the Brisbane coast.

In his first full year as a tournament pro, Norman made the top five of the Australian Order of Merit table, and that qualified him to compete on the European circuit. He arrived in Britain in 1977, having won a Japanese tournament en route, and immediately established himself as one of the most exciting young players on the tour.

For the next five years, professional golf in Europe provided fascinating competition. The fledgling European circuit was raw in many ways, compared with the richly endowed and efficient US Tour. There was no great depth of playing quality, but the annual battle for supremacy was intense – and the golf, I insist, was often the best being played on any circuit in the world. Norman regularly won two or three tournaments a year, although only once, in 1982, did he take the title of European No. 1. His international reputation, founded on two victories in the World Match Play Championship, was enhanced by successes in his increasing world travels, with wins in Fiji and Hong Kong and dominance of his home circuit.

Last year, he decided that he was ready for America and had already taken unto himself an American wife, sired a daughter and moved into an upmarket development in Florida.

At the Bay Hill Classic, Norman tied for first and was beaten in a sudden-death playoff by an absurdly rash putt and Mike Nicolette. It is always a matter of some delicacy knowing what to say to a friend who has just blown a winning chance, and a long friendship with Ben Crenshaw has not taught me a diplomatic turn of phrase for the occasion. My trepidation was groundless. Norman sought me out and said, 'Come and look at something.' The something was a blood-red Ferrari that had just been delivered, an event of much greater importance in Norman's mind than losing a playoff. He is an unabashed car-perv, in his phrase, and his stable contains two Rolls-Royces, plus sundry high-performance beasts. On this occasion, my envy was expressed in a caustic question about what shall it profit a man to own a Ferrari in a country with a 55-mile-per-hour speed limit, not counting a reasonable tolerance on the part of the highway patrol.

Norman completely ruined my day by saying that he had an arrangement with a racetrack and could give his hairy monsters their head anytime he liked. My guess is that he will soon start flying lessons.

A few more guesses are in order at this stage of his career as, at the age of twenty-nine, he is poised at the crossroads. Will he take the Pilgrim's Progress path to greatness and spiritual fulfilment? Or will he be diverted into the lush byways of winning millions of dollars without causing a flutter among the record books? Well, I will wager my Scottish castle, my Black Forest shooting estate, twenty of my most attentive handmaidens that he will win at least one major championship. Beyond that I would prefer to hedge my bets. It all depends on that core of ambition and determination residing so deeply within him that even he cannot unravel its secrets.

Those who know him best are equally ambivalent about his potential. Every golfer respects his ability, but, in the rarified level that we are discussing, technique is 10 per cent of the game, at most. Australians are notoriously reluctant to find a good word about their fellow countrymen. Peter Thomson, five times the British Open Champion, has serious reservations about Greg Norman's capacity to go all the way in golf. Jack Newton refers to him as 'The Great White Fish Finger'. Graham Marsh, on the other hand, believes that Norman will improve further and become a truly dominant figure. It is, of course, best that we do not know because life would be arid without the mystery. It is enough to know of the rich rewards to be had from watching Norman's progress, win or lose.

Peter's caution proved to be sensible. To date, Greg has indeed won 'at least one major championship'. Two, in fact.

(GOLF DIGEST 1984)

What's the matter with Greg Norman?

His height, about seven feet at a conservative estimate, is not the most impressive physical feature about him. He has to edge sideways through a standard, three-foot doorway and those Li'l Abner shoulders taper to a 34-inch waist.

He is routinely described by journalists as resembling a Nordic god on the basis that he has a Finnish mother and fair hair.

After travelling extensively through the United States, he concluded that the best possible place to live would be on the east coast of an English-speaking enclave of Florida, preferably close to his good friend Jack Nicklaus.

Accordingly, he built his dream house in the millionaire's sanctuary of North Palm Beach, a convenient location for deep-sea fishing. He had become addicted to this form of recreation in his native Australia off the Great Barrier Reef.

He has a beautiful and charming wife who has given him two happy and healthy children. All are devoted to each other.

He is a self-confessed car-perv. Unlike most motoring enthusiasts, who have to live out their fantasies through the pages of magazines, he is able to indulge his ambitions. At the last count, he owned a Rolls-Royce, two Ferraris, an Aston Martin and sundry mundane runabouts, Cadillacs or whatever, for dropping the children off at school.

Through his close friendship with Nigel Mansell, the Ferrari Grand Prix driver and near world champion in 1987, he is able to drive the most potent machinery on racing circuits and take part in saloon-car competitions.

His first sporting love, however, is golf, a game he found ludicrously easy from the day he took it up as a boy. He had success the day he began to compete in tournaments and has averaged better than four victories a year since he turned pro in 1976.

He won the British Open at Turnberry in 1986 and freakish luck, either freakishly good luck in the case of rivals or freakishly bad luck on his own part, cost him four other major victories.

He laughed off those disappointments as 'one of those things' and thereby enhanced his reputation as one of the premier ambassadors for sportsmanship.

As an enthusiast of golf, he would be prepared to make considerable sacrifices for the chance to play. In his case sacrifices are not necessary. Sponsors willingly pay him in excess of $1 million a year just to persuade him to enter their tournaments. They send their executive jets to fetch him. They put him up at the finest hotels and shower him with luxurious gifts. His slightest whim is instantly gratified, any diversion arranged.

During this 'down time', he is not constrained by the thoughts that nag at, say, a freelance golf writer, that he is spending money like water and not earning a penny. The cornucopia of mixed currencies continues to pour into his pockets even while his tailored trousers are hanging in the closet as he sleeps.

If the sun is excessively hot, he does not buy a hat like the rest of us. He calls his manager. On the instant, a load of hats arrives for his approval. Of course, there is an invoice, but it is not from the milliner with the usual suggestion that early payment would be appreciated. It is from him to the milliner, to the effect that, sure, he does not mind wearing the Indiana Jones model, in specified parts of the world, provided the wind is not so strong that the wearing of a hat is inconvenient, for the consideration of half a million clams per annum. This same marketing exercise is applied to every part of his body, or very nearly.

Of course, he is subject to all the worries and crises that beset the rest of us. The same income tax demand flops onto his mat in due season. His kids catch the usual juvenile germs. His wife is driven to distraction because she cannot get matching materials for the kitchen curtains. The neighbour's dog is using the back lawn for antisocial purposes. Barely pausing as he strides to the garage to take one of the Ferraris for its morning rip up the turnpike, he solves all these problems without turning a hair: 'Get my office onto it.'

One thing puzzles me. Why do people keep asking the question again and again: 'What's the matter with Greg Norman?'

This column was somewhat reminiscent of the old George Best joke – the one about the room-service waiter who goes up to the wayward soccer star's lavish suite with champagne and caviar and finds his hero partaking of certain substances in bed with three Miss Worlds. 'Tell me, Mr Best,' he says, as he puts the tray down, 'where did it all go wrong?'

For Norman, the car count has doubtless changed, and he has added a second Open Championship, at Royal St George's in 1993, to his first – and with a major championship record low aggregate of 267. However, he has also since completed a record of having lost all four majors in a playoff. And at the 1996 Masters, a six-shot lead after 54 holes turned into a five-shot defeat at the hands of Nick Faldo. Nevertheless, as with the George Best anecdote, Dobereiner's question makes a point.

(GOLF DIGEST 1990)

The other Mr Norman

The crowd behind the eighteenth green cheered as the leader's approach shot smacked into the turf. The ball took two hops and then reversed under the effect of backspin, finishing three feet from the flag. The leader, now with three strokes for victory, walked briskly on to the green and deliberately clipped the ball into a bunker with his putter.

He splashed the ball back onto the green and, with his usual perfunctory glance along the line, stroked it into the hole.

Can you name the golfer? Well, a bit more of the story. With radio reporters vamping madly and promising to have the winner at the microphone any minute now, and with distraught tournament officials unable to delay the presentation ceremony any longer, the hero of the hour was hiding in a toilet until the hullabaloo died down and he could slip away quietly into the night in his battered old Cadillac.

You may never have heard of him, but mention that incident, or a hundred more like it, to any of the great players in North America and identification will be instantaneous.

'It could only be Moe Norman.' They speak his name with awe, and affection, and amused exasperation, and sometimes with a hint of envy, for Norman is blessed with a talent for striking a golf ball which is as legendary as his eccentricity.

Ever since I first began to hear weird and wonderful tales of Norman, I have been trying to track him down, but he is a will-o'-the-wisp character. Where do you start looking for a man who habitually sleeps in his car, who keeps on the move and is so suspicious of strangers that he refuses to entrust his money to a bank?

Moe drifted into golf the way most boys of his generation did, by hanging around a golf club and earning pocket money as a caddie. The club in question was in Kitchener, Ontario, and Moe was coached by the pro, Lloyd Tucker, who was responsible for bringing on quite a few fine Canadian players.

The one element which Tucker did not drill into Norman was a classical style. All his life Norman has stood to the ball stiff-legged, knees braced back, with a pronounced stoop from the waist and with his hands as far from his body as he could get them with fully stretched arms.

His impact on Canadian amateur golf was sensational. He would not have a caddie, remarking, 'Bag's not heavy, bag's not heavy,' much to the tight-lipped disapproval of established figures in the Royal Canadian Golf Association. He won everything, Canadian Amateur Championships and provincial championships, seemingly as he pleased.

The town of Kitchener turned out in force to hail the local hero at a Moe Norman night, with the full ceremonial of civic speeches, presentation and fanfares. Needless to say, Norman did not turn up.

In match play events, he often conceded ten-foot putts – 'that's good, that's good' – and then won the hole by rolling home his fifteen-footers, a devastating psychological gambit which finally left opponents unable to hole the vital two-footer and which stood him in good stead in his coming career among the rich pigeons.

Lesser amateur tournaments put up the usual prizes such as TV sets, furniture and other household appliances. Norman won four rocking-chair first prizes in successive years. He began to get cute, and it was at this time that he learned how to produce the exact score he needed, a facility later to win him many bets as a gypsy pro touring the resort courses down South. He would ask around if anyone wanted to buy a radio, for instance, and then, having made the deal and set the price, he would contrive to finish in the place which carried the radio as the prize.

Officialdom frowned on such covert professionalism, drawing from Norman the classic response: 'What do you do with twenty-seven toasters?'

However, Norman was persuaded to do the decent thing and turn pro. He made the Canadian PGA Championship virtually a Moe Norman benefit, but in other professional events he sometimes seemed completely uninterested.

'Don't know if I want to win. Just a walk in the park, just a walk in the park.'

Eventually, Norman was persuaded much against his inclinations to venture into the big pond of the American tour. He was so overawed at first that his main interest was in diffidently asking the star players for their autographs. His friend Bert Turcotte was exasperated: 'Moe, what the hell are you doing? You're out here to whip these guys' asses.'

'Me?' said Norman in astonishment at the idea. 'Oh, no. I'm not supposed to beat them.'

Norman is a Coca-Cola addict and at the Los Angeles Open he walked onto the first tee carrying a bottle, which he placed on the turf. Then, to the delight of the gallery, he put his ball on the top of the bottle and drove off. On another occasion, he balanced his ball on a pyramid tee marker and drove off from that. Sometimes, to relieve the tedium of practice rounds, he would throw down a ball and leap into the shot while the ball was still rolling, cracking it 250 yards down the middle.

At Augusta, Norman made history as the only player ever to walk out of the Masters. He had caused something of a stir behind the scenes by sacking the caddie allotted to him before the poor man had even picked up the bag and then, when a breeze blew up for the third round with Norman in fifth position, he said, 'Too windy for golf. Back to Canada, back to Canada,' and disappeared.

Norman and the big time were clearly incompatible and mutually happy to end the association. For one thing, it was not too good for the image of professional golf to have a player striking side bets with the gallery, such as whether he could keep a ball bouncing on his club face as he walked along the fairway (his record was 193 bounces) or whether he could get down from a bunker in two strokes with one hand.

For me, Norman's greatest claim to fame lay in one of his favourite sidelines. When opportunity arose, or could be contrived, he would strike a wager that he could break the course record, without even having seen the course. He has collected on seventeen such bets to date and on this particular occasion was playing with the local pro. He came to the last needing a four to win his wager and asked the other pro what kind of hole it was. 'Drive and 9-iron,' he was told. Norman took out his 9-iron and hit the ball off the tee, following it with a full driver shot off the fairway to the flag for a birdie three.

If you are ever in Ontario (in summer) or Florida when the snow makes golf impossible in Canada and a scruffy, portly man in his early fifties asks if you would like a game of golf with a little bit of interest on the side, settle for a wager you can well afford to lose and jump at the opportunity. You might just be in for a golf lesson from one of the game's consummate masters.

(GUARDIAN 1981)

Will the real Lee Trevino please stand up?

He was scowling as he walked into tournament headquarters. Everything about him was belligerent. The way he walked, the way he thrust a slip of paper at the receptionist, proclaimed him as a man determined to show that he was as good as the next man in order to silence the private inner voice which suggested that he might not be.

I didn't hear what they were saying, but the tone was unmistakable. The voice which I later came to know so well was pitched somewhere between a bark and a whine. Their discussion was brief and soon his squat, paunchy figure was marching out of the room. He was looking straight ahead, still with that thunderstorm frown. The chip on his shoulder was almost visible. What a charming specimen, I thought.

'Who was that?' I asked.

'That gentleman,' said the receptionist with heavy sarcasm, 'was Mr Lee Trevino.'

'I never heard of him,' I said.

'You've just been lucky,' she answered.

Later that day, I was at the practice ground and saw Trevino hitting balls. I cast an appraising eye over his swing and was not impressed by that, either. You must understand that we professional golf watchers develop an instinct about these things. Obviously, it is not possible to keep tabs on three hundred golfers, so when a new one comes along we size him up and decide whether he is one to watch in the future.

I gave Trevino no chance. He was striking the ball well enough, but they all do on the practice ground. Could he be an original, like Doug Sanders, Gay Brewer or Miller Barber, who could repeat that swing under pressure? (You will gather that I am not a slave to orthodoxy or the classic style. I don't mind how anybody hits the ball so long as he can keep on hitting it that way when the going gets tough.)

Trevino's flat, lunging style did not fill me with confidence. He gave the impression of a man who was not so much interested in practising his golf as working off some deep grudge against the balls. He was punishing them. Or, more accurately, he was identifying the balls with people and getting his own back.

'Take that, you smart-ass receptionist! Take that, you sneering locker-room attendant!' Trevino was hitting back at the whole world.

Get him out on the course needing to finish 4–4–3 for the tournament, I thought, and that swing will collapse into the biggest hook you ever saw. As a crosscheck on my judgment, I looked up his record. He was nearly thirty and had never even threatened to win anything. That figured. There was no need to take any further notice of Lee Trevino.

So much for first impressions. In my own defence I may add that many an experienced professional came to the same conclusions about Trevino and his swing in those days.

Now let us move the story along a bit and introduce a totally different character. By coincidence his name was also Lee Trevino. He had won the US Open Championship, and he was sitting in the press tent, relaxed and happy. He was everybody's friend. The jokes – good, bad, clean, vulgar – poured from him like a pro comic trying to do the routines of a lifetime in half an hour. The crowds at the practice ground had been treated to a similar performance. And even on the course, with thousands of dollars at stake, he had gagged with the galleries all the way round.

He may be as shallow as a dirty limerick, we told ourselves, but he is a lovable guy and terrific company away from the course. He knows how to live. The breweries will have to go on overtime while he is in the money, and everybody had better lock up their daughters.

Then, a bit later, I met another Lee Trevino. On this occasion, it was a business meeting and I was involved in the production of an instructional series with him. He was all business. Before I could finish a question he was ahead of me, rattling out the answer and directing the photographer to get the correct angles. The nearest he came to a joke was when he was explaining his conception of the two-piece swing.

'I usually tell people I have a two-piece method because, being a Mexican, I'm not smart enough to count up to three.'

He gave a thin, conspiratorial smile. The crowds expect jokes so jokes is what they get. This was a different situation.

It was different in other ways, too. Trevino revealed himself as a profound thinker about the techniques of golf. Everyone knew him to be a canny player by now, plotting his way round a golf course in strict accordance with his prearranged plan.

The refreshing part about Trevino's theorizing was its originality. Nobody ever showed him how to hold a club or make a backswing. That all came as a result of lonely hours of trial and error as a boy. So, when he eventually came to pick up a textbook, he already knew the answers because he had worked out the proofs. From his own experience he could say 'Rubbish!' to much of the book lore of golf technique.

By the same token he totally rejected most of the concepts of good swings and bad swings.

'Who can dare say I have a bad swing?' he asked. 'The only thing that matters in golf is the scores you put on the board. You don't have to look pretty out there, you have to win. Look at my record and tell me who has a better swing than mine.'

There could be no arguing with the logic of his view. Since 1968, he had scored lower and earned higher than any golfer save, in some respects, Jack Nicklaus. And in direct confrontation with Nicklaus, as in the play-off for the 1971 US Open at Merion, Trevino came out best.

There is even another Trevino, the family man who wants

nothing more than to watch his children grow up. But that can be left out of the present discussion. Three Lee Trevinos are enough to be going on with. And the central question to be resolved is quite simple. Which is the real one?

Is it that surly fellow with the crashing inferiority complex? Is it the knock-about comic? Is it the down-to-earth student of golf?

The first thing to remember is that Trevino was a shanty-poor, fatherless Mexican during his Texas childhood, which is one way of saying that the world regarded him as a second-class citizen. Trevino resented the poverty and the prejudice, as all of his kind must. We should not be surprised that people everywhere, who are denied all privileges, react against the system and sometimes fall into crime. Society ought to be gaoled but, of course, it is society which has the impertinence to do the gaoling.

Trevino did not fall into crime, but he deeply wanted to find an identity. What could be more natural than for such a boy to seek the group identity of that rip-roaring, two-fisted body, the US Marines?

As a Marine, Trevino found self-respect and the respect of society. From a nobody he became one of the élite, and soon enough his prowess as a golfer made him an élite member of the élite group. With security came confidence and with confidence his golf became even better.

Serving in the Far East helped. At home there had been daily reminders that he was regarded as an inferior. But now he found himself as an American in countries where Americans were acknowledged, especially by themselves, as superiors. At a stroke, Trevino had gone from about four down to at least two up.

In this environment, his natural talents, notably a quick intelligence and a ready wit, could flourish and develop. And it soon came to Trevino that if he could be a big fish in the small pond of the Marines, why couldn't he be an even bigger fish in the pond of professional golf? What he forgot – or thought he could lick – was that as soon as he took off his uniform and came home he would revert to being a *Chicano* so far as society was concerned.

Once again, life was tough for him. But now he was better equipped to handle the tensions. The game of golf had mush-roomed to such a degree that an ability to break par was potentially the passport which would break down all barriers. Talking would get him only so far – after that his clubs would have to take over the conversation.

Compared with the college scholarship golfers, and even the elevated caddies, Trevino started his pro career at a consider-able disadvantage. But in another sense, his unorthodox apprenticeship was an invaluable experience. He was like a boxer without any coach, or trainer, or fancy gymnasium to practise his moves. He was straight into the fairground booth, knowing that he had to win to eat. He learned all the tricks.

'When you are playing for five bucks and you've got two bucks in your pocket – that's pressure,' he said later, when someone complimented him on his composure in sinking his Open Championship putts.

'Where's the pressure when you've got a five-footer for the Open? Hole it or miss it, you still wind up with a pocket full of dollars.'

He hustled and bustled his way to a big local reputation in Texas. And then, when he finally made it onto the professional tour, he found that the big boys knew most of the tricks, too. Trevino struggled, and he admits that after a bit he was ready to pack up and return to the minor league golf of local tourna-ments, keeping shop and accommodating any member or visitor rash enough to put out a challenge. He knew he could make a good living that way. On the tour all he was doing was spending his nest egg of hard-won five-dollar bets.

Eventually, as the world knows, his wife used her own savings to enter him for the US Open and he went along to please her. It was to be his last fling at the big time. And he won.

With victory came what seemed to be that remarkable transformation in his character. In reality, all that changed was his bank balance. The exuberant personality had been there all the time but, as he put it, 'You don't feel like kidding around too much when you are living on fish heads and rice.'

That win was the trigger which released all his inhibitions. The preamble to the Constitution of the United States declares that all men are born free and equal. After thirty years, Trevino had finally given some kind of validity to that lofty ideal. He was free and equal. Aided and abetted by his then manager, the improbable Bucky Woy, he rode his new image hard. A bit too hard for the taste of some, and rather more than he himself felt to be natural.

He likes to make jokes, which is something very different from having to make jokes because people expect it. And, as he consolidated his success, he grew confident enough to please himself rather than others. If he felt low, he could be low. If he felt chipper, he could gag it up.

He has still, I think, not quite emancipated himself entirely. After all, the gay caballero image is a valuable trading asset and must be preserved. Trevino contrived a remarkable self-discipline along the lines of that useful American TV accessory, the blab-off. This is a switch on a long flex which enables the viewer to switch off the advertisements without moving from his chair. On the golf course Trevino's personal blab-off enables him to chatter and gag with the crowd as he walks between shots and then, at a touch of a switch, as it were, give his total concentration to the shot in hand.

Even though security is assured for life, Trevino is still not above pulling a stroke. Jack Nicklaus diplomatically denied that he had been put off when Trevino produced an imitation snake on the first tee at Merion. Indeed, he said, the incident had helped to break his tension. All I know is that it scared the daylights out of me, and I was only watching.

Trevino is also a master of gamesmanship. Put him in a play-off with a young golfer and he openly boasts that he will 'psych' him out of it. And he does, of that there is no doubt.

So, in response to the demand for the real Trevino to stand up, all three of our original nominees rise to their feet. The morose Mexican has mellowed with success, but he can still show that face from time to time. The scars of a background like Trevino's never entirely heal. The brash comic has also become diluted. Trevino has given up drinking entirely, and these days the jokes are not forced. He gags when the spirit moves him and his wit is the sharper for it. As for the thoughtful Trevino, he is coming more and more into his own. He is the one I like best, and I look forward to the day when this Trevino is entirely dominant. I think you will like him – he is a very interesting fellow.

Prior to the appearance of this article, Trevino had won both major Open Championships twice – in America in 1968 and 1971 and in Britain in 1971 and 1972. He then went on to win the USPGA Championship in 1974 and 1984. Once he turned fifty, he carved out another highly lucrative career on the US Senior tour. But the reference to Bucky Woy is instructive. Trevino had not had the best of financial fortune with his past managers until he joined his present one, Chuck Rubin, brother-in-law to Tom Watson. Trevino has made a lot of money, and he has lost a lot.

(GOLF WORLD 1973)

Not a teetotal champion

When Christy O'Connor was the professional at Bundoran in Co. Donegal, long before he became a tournament player, he played a regular four-ball match with three low-handicap members. On one occasion, an opponent asked what club he had hit on the downhill par-3 thirteenth, which measured 235 yards. On being informed that Christy had used his 3-iron, the member announced proudly, 'I hit a 5-iron!'

Irish golf is waged to the accompaniment of a fierce barrage of witty banter, or *craic* in the Gaelic, hence the term 'wise crack', and Christy's partner was quick with a verbal thrust to deflate the braggart, adding that the numbers engraved on the clubs mean nothing to Christy; he could play the hole with any club in the bag.

Next to insulting each other, the Irish like nothing better than taking a punt or two off each other with a little flutter. A wager is a serious matter, involving a debt of honour no less, and so Christy was forced into a demonstration. He hit a ball onto the green with every club in his bag, including the putter. I wonder how many of today's superstars could do the same.

Peter Alliss was Christy's regular foursome partner in the Ryder Cup and still cannot believe one of the shots he played. Alliss had driven and the ball finished in a deep divot scrape on a pronounced downslope. He just could not imagine what kind of shot could be contrived to advance the ball any distance. Christy showed not the slightest concern, announcing, 'I think I'll give it a cut with the driver.' Alliss watched in dumbfounded fascination as the ball went off like a rocket, to finish six feet from the distant flagstick.

An even greater shot, certainly a nominee for the most remarkable golf stroke ever made, was played by Christy in the 1963 World (Canada) Cup at St Nom la Breteche, near Paris. He does not like to talk about this one because he had, as the Irish say, drink taken. There is no expression in Ireland, either in the Gaelic or English languages, to convey an excess of alcohol. A man may be said to be 'full', or to have had 'enough'. It is impossible for a man to have had 'too much' to drink. Such a notion would be ludicrous hyperbole, like saying that a girl was too beautiful or the rain too wet.

Suffice to say that play was impossible because thick fog enveloped the golf course and much the same could be said of Christy after he had spent the entire day and most of the night in the bar. At one point, a man who incurred Christy's displeasure left the room backwards at high speed without observing the formality of opening the door.

Thus, it came about that the golf correspondent of the London *Evening Standard*, Mark Wilson, came across Christy in the locker room next morning, groaning softly and grappling with the eternal problem which has confounded men in his condition since the dawn of civilization, namely: Which shoe goes on which foot? Also: How can I bend over to pick up the selected shoe without having my head explode and spatter the room with molten lava?

Wilson solved the shoe dilemma in a trice and eased Christy into the vertical mode. Christy steadied himself by grasping Wilson around the throat with both hands. 'Get a large jug of strong, black coffee with a dart of the hair of the dog in it. I leave the size of the measure to your discretion. Pace off 250 yards up the right side of the first hole and wait for me 20 yards into the woods.' With that, he teetered gingerly to the first tee.

The crowd's reaction to Christy's sliced drive was an embarrassed silence. As Wilson waited in the depths of a French wood, he felt that he had been sent on a fool's errand. Nobody could nominate a shot with such precision, certainly nobody who was barely capable of standing upright. Crash! The ball ripped into the canopy and fell dutifully at Wilson's feet. Christy followed in due course and drained the jug. He went on to score 68, four under par, while certainly one over the eight.

Christy is a difficult man to place in the pecking order of the golfing greats because his record lacks a single major championship. But you have only to see that fluid, self-taught swing to appreciate that this is no first-class second-rater but a man to be numbered among the very best in the history of golf.

He is by nature a reserved, very private man, and while he would have liked the professional satisfaction of winning an Open, he would have hated the lionizing and speechifying which goes with being the champion golfer. His style is a couple of jars and a bit of *craic* with the lads and then home to supper with his beloved Mary.

(GOLF WORLD 1993)

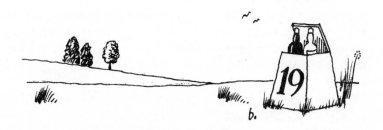

Daly must find his own salvation

There can be no denying that John Daly has brought the profession of golf into disrepute. Repeatedly so. He has put up a black, blotted his copybook, let the side down, embarrassed his fellow professionals by making a frightful ass of himself and so on, and so on.

He has been brought to book, hauled over the coals, put on a fizzer, marched up before the beak, carpeted and castigated and given numerous rockets. He has, one has to admit, accepted his various punishments without demur.

He has scrutinized his ways and in the areas where he found them to be defect, he has mended them. The manner in which he has rehabilitated himself from the depths of dipsomania is certainly highly commendable and deserving of continued encouragement.

These days, golf is much more vigilant in enforcing the rules and monitoring standards of deportment and behaviour, which is just as well since a lapse into the unsporting ethic which is increasingly infecting other popular sports would leave us without a game to play. It is impossible for an angry man or a dishonest man to play golf properly, although some still try it on.

One competitor in a recent British Open was disqualified, and subsequently banned from professional golf for forty-five years. When the referee was asked by how much the player had been moving his marker on the green, he answered that it would have to be measured in fractions of a mile rather than fractions of a foot.

A Ryder Cup captain ordered his team not to help look for American balls in the rough and, when the players protested, he sheepishly sought to justify his unsporting command by saying he was afraid of penalties for accidentally moving an opponent's ball. (There is, of course, no penalty if you accidentally move an opponent's ball during a search.)

In a subsequent, foursomes match, a player refused to help search for his own ball. He carved his approach shot deep into the jungle and then sat down on his golf bag and rested while his partner and their opponents went off to hunt for the ball.

The knowledge that your behaviour on the course is liable to be relayed to the TV screens in 20 million homes, including the one watched by your wife and children, is undoubtedly a restraining influence on today's players.

Some of the game's more colourful characters simply could not have played tournament golf in today's conditions. There was one who released his internal pressures of frustration and disgust by head-butting trees, kicking himself on the shins and, on one occasion, knocking himself out with a self-inflicted left hook. One of his contemporaries who was waiting to drive off was the target of some wounding verbal abuse from a spectator. The player turned his back on his tormentor, bent over and broke wind, effectively ending further discussion.

I had planned to offer a substantial cash reward from my personal fortune for the first reader to submit an all-correct list identifying the heroes of the above incidents. To my deep disappointment it has been officially deemed that any such competition would jeopardize the amateur status of everyone involved. That would never do.

Please note that John Daly has never done anything as reprehensible as these examples. For all I know he may have grown a beard at some time but that is no longer among the offences officially designated by the PGA as bringing the profession into disrepute.

Few of us can aspire to the level of moral rectitude of the lady captain of Effingham Golf Club, near London. Her 4-ball was putting out when a naked flasher leapt out of the bushes. The lady captain fixed him with a laser stare and in tones of righteous outrage demanded, 'Are you a member?'

The pathetic pervert was stopped in his tracks by the incongruity of the question, giving the lady captain time to make the appropriate club selection (she opted for a 5-iron) and despatch the wretch with a well-directed blow to his dignity.

But we can all try to protect the game by doing our best to play by the spirit and letter of the law. Let our example rather than verbal outbursts of indignant censure show the malefactors the error of their ways. Daly is trying his hardest. I suggest that we all get off his case and leave him to find his own salvation.

This was written just a few months after Daly had won his second major championship, the Open at St Andrews. He has had his problems with the demon drink since, though at the last checking he was devoutly sober again.

(GOLF WORLD 1996)

The Knickers Man

The Americans called him The Knickers Man, a hugely amusing joke to his more vulgar friends in the golfing fraternity because women's panties are known as knickers in Britain and the young Max Faulkner had a formidable reputation as a Casanova.

He was a striking figure on the golf course, tall and handsome, his athletic figure accentuated by his invariable dress of plus-twos in pastel shades with colour co-ordinated shirt, stockings and shoes. At fifty he boasted that his waist measurement was the same as it was when he boxed as a middleweight thirty years earlier. Even today at seventy-nine he stands as erect and trim as a guardsman.

Faulkner's peacock finery was in sharp contrast, and deliberately so, to the appearance of his caddie, Mad Mac, who wore a tie but no shirt under several layers of voluminous overcoats. He carried a pair of opera glasses, from which the lenses had long since vanished, through which he studied the lines of Faulkner's putts while lying flat on the green. As often as not he would offer the advice: 'Hit it slightly straight, Sir.'

The theatrical quality of the partnership's appearance was matched by Faulkner's flair as a dramatist, a gift he exploited fully to promote his career. In an era when the professionals dressed so that they would melt into the background and rationed their public utterances to 'You're up' and 'Good hit', Faulkner was a godsend to the golfing press. He stole the headlines even when he missed the cut.

For example, at an Irish Open at Woodbrook, near Dublin,

Faulkner was holding court in the bar at 11 p.m. when two writers from London evening papers told him that they had to produce early edition stories at 8.15 the next morning and they had nothing to write about. Max allayed their fears. 'I am in the 8 a.m. group tomorrow. Just be there by the first tee.' They were.

As Faulkner was about to drive off, a small boy in the gallery cried out, 'Dad, Dad, can I speak to you?'

'Let the boy through,' commanded Max.

'Dad, I have to leave today and go back to school. But I have lost all my money, every penny. What shall I do?'

The crowd cheered as Faulkner pulled out his wallet with a flourish, removed every note and handed the wad to the boy. 'Off you go, son,' he ordered, 'and don't be late for school.' With that he held up his wallet upside-down and shook it, to emphasize that he had kept nothing back for himself. 'See. I am broke. Now I have to win.' He didn't, but he ended the day with bigger headlines than the man who did.

One of the golf writers who benefited from this charade was Mark Wilson of the London *Evening Standard*. Some time later, he went to interview Faulkner at his farm in Sussex and on the way he passed a recovery vehicle retrieving Faulkner's crumpled E-type Jaguar from a ditch. It transpired that Faulkner had been driving home at his usual breakneck speed from a golf club dinner in the early hours of the morning when the car skidded on a steep hill, hit the nearside kerbstone, careened across the road and hit the other kerb, flipped over a hedge without touching it, landed on its roof and and slithered 50 yards through a wood. Faulkner regained consciousness, wrapped around the steering wheel and pinioned by the crushed roof, with blood streaming from a head wound.

His only possible way of escape was to dig a rut in the hillside with his heels and wriggle clear feet first. He staggered for a mile and half and then managed to wake the landlord of a pub. When Wilson arrived at the farm later that morning, Faulkner answered the door, his head swathed in bandages.

'You can write that I have now retired from tournaments,' he said. 'Have to. No wheels to travel. I've written off so many cars that I refuse to buy another.'

Six hours later, Wilson's notebook was full of a celebration of Faulkner's career. As he was leaving, Faulkner said, 'Would you mind giving me a hand?' He led the way to a barn. In a dark corner was a mound shrouded beneath a tarpaulin which was covered with an accretion of years of chicken droppings. They pulled it clear to reveal a shiny Alfa Romeo saloon. 'I thought I had one somewhere,' commented Max.

The career was resumed, even unto the age of fifty-two, when he became the oldest man to win an Open Championship by adding the Portuguese Open to his tally of victories, the greatest of which, of course, was the British Open at Portrush in 1951. He tried more than three hundred putters during his tournament life, quite a few of them made by himself. Adhesives were not as reliable as today's epoxy and bits used to fall off. But that week in Northern Ireland, he had one which suited him perfectly. He had rounds of 27, 24 and 29 putts and then, on his way to the first tee for the final circuit, he had the temerity to sign a golf ball for a little boy: 'Max Faulkner, Open champion.' Twenty-nine more putts and he justified his braggadocio. In his interview, he held out his hands and announced, 'I am never going to miss one of those again for the rest of my life.' Henry Longhurst wrote that at this point he moved away, lest the gods mistook him for an accomplice in this blasphemy.

Faulkner's madcap lifestyle of roistering, boozing and tearaway driving was as much an inheritance as the hereditary complaint called familial tremors which today afflicts his hands. His father, Gus, was a giant of a man who was apprenticed to James Braid at three shillings and sixpence a week. He developed into a gifted player and an immensely strong one. He hit with such power that the name of the ball became imprinted in mirror image on the face of his rusty irons. Braid made him play off plus-8 and he still won prizes.

His career was interrupted and fatally compromised by World War I, when he was invalided back from Flanders suffering from shell shock, the only survivor from his howitzer battery. After the war, he took an appointment as professional at a club in Wales and when he won the Welsh Championship a grateful government reduced his war disability pension by 50 per cent.

Gus Faulkner's elder son, Frank, was killed serving with the Welsh Guards in World War II, but Max was fortunate enough to spend most of his RAF service guarding the underground command post of Winston Churchill and General Eisenhower at Wentworth Golf Club.

He had started to play golf at the age of four and he developed a huge over-swing, hitting himself on the leg with the club-head on both the backswing and the follow-through. Gus recognized that the boy was a natural and left him to find his own golfing salvation, apart from offering the odd tip. Max practised daily until driven in by darkness, a habit of diligence which commended him to Henry Cotton, who engaged him as his assistant.

In order to further Max's ambitions and provide him with good practice facilities, Gus bought Selsey Golf Club on the south coast of England. In due season, Max invested his life savings in the creation of West Chiltington Golf Club so that his son-in-law, Brian Barnes, could have a secure golfing base. Max retired from his second career, as a professional fisherman, to become the club's mole-catcher.

He made his first return to Portrush (now Royal) since his Open Championship triumph forty-four years earlier to watch Barnes play in the British Seniors Championship. 'That was the worst pressure of my life, having the old chap watching me and willing me to uphold the family honour at Portrush.' He won, despite a nervous three putts on the last green.

Every week, Max's old Ryder Cup colleague, Ken Bousfield, drives down from London to West Chiltington for a game. The tremor in Faulkner's hands does not affect his full shots and he still gives the ball a dirty great wallop. The short putts, though, are not a pretty sight.

The swashbuckling Knickers Man sometimes wishes that he had accepted Bobby Locke's invitation to join him on his cherry-picking invasion of America in 1947 because he was the better player at that time, though he acknowledges that Locke had the more even temperament, and Locke really cleaned up on those trips. Faulkner stayed at home because of his enduring attachment to home, wife, Joan, and family.

Looking back over a lifetime packed with lurid, breathtaking, glorious and disastrous incidents, his one serious regret is that the nation has never acknowledged his Open Championship achievement with a medal, even a modest one, in the Honours List. That is an oversight which brings discredit to successive British governments.

Although this piece has not previously been published, that wasn't because it was rejected. It was one Peter had been working on in the summer of 1996 which had not yet been submitted for publication.

Gerald the Great

An era in golf ended last weekend with the death at the age of seventy-seven of Gerald Micklem, the game's only authentic oracle on this side of the Atlantic; although his friend and counterpart in America, Joe Dey, happily remains with us.

This is not to say that the two men operated like territorial animals, confining their oracular operations to their own spheres of influence. Dey was elected captain of the Royal and Ancient Club of St Andrews, as Micklem had been, and the name 'Gerald' was like a password all over the world.

For forty years or so anyone who was anyone in golf knew, or knew of, this legendary figure. Very, very few of them ever came close to a passable impersonation of his speech, let alone his acid wit. The plummy Eton and Christnose vowels, actually Winchester and Trinity, were compressed into a Brigade of Guards bark and delivered at high pitch and even higher speed, as they had to be to keep pace with his fertile intellect.

When he made a speech on receiving the Donald Ross award from the American Society of Golf Course Architects, the company rose for an ovation and my neighbour remarked, 'That was absolutely fabulous; I didn't understand a single word he said.'

In one sense Gerald was a golfing archetype of his time and class. His Oxford blue gave him an entrée into the City, which in turn enabled him to pursue an active amateur career as an English international, Walker Cup regular and twice English champion. Some care must be taken in assessing his stature as a player because he loathed sycophancy and would have hated the idea of having it laid on too thickly when he was no longer able to administer an astringent corrective.

For a quarter of a century I have stiffened to the Caterham Barracks yelp of 'Golf writer! Git it wrong again on Sunday.' He then put me right on a point of fact or interpretation and, to my shame, it was some time before I penetrated the layers of tribal camouflage with which this breed of Englishman conceals his feelings and realized that he was motivated by a genuine spirit of helpfulness.

Years later, when I had learnt how to read his conversational wrong 'uns and understood that kindness and generosity were the keys to his character, I asked him if he would read the manuscript of a book I had written (*Golf Rules Explained*, seventh edition hot off the presses, order now while stocks last).

All my publisher wanted, as Gerald well understood, was the Micklem imprimatur as former chairman of the Rules of Golf committee. He went through the manuscript word by word and his forthright marginal notations were so revealing that I had to do an extensive rewrite.

So, there must be no sloppy hyperbole in assessing Gerald's golf. He himself would probably have settled for some throwaway expression such as 'a pretty useful performer on his day', but he had to be better than that when he won the English in 1953, beating Ronnie White, whom Arnold Palmer reckons the best amateur he has seen.

We are on surer ground in measuring Gerald when he reached the stage of social golf and annual competitive flings in the Oxford and Cambridge Society's competition for the President's Putter, retired from the Stock Exchange and devoted his life to administration.

By the conventions of his background, he should have become an Establishment figure, a committee time-server inheriting the high offices of the game on the basis of Buggins' turn and gradually declining into the state of pompous, old buffer, or elder statesman as it is more politely known.

Publicly, he played that part but behind the scenes – and he was behind all the golf scenes – he was a maverick. Golf administration in those days was like a committee meeting of the Athenaeum, life being ordered along the unchanging lines that had been followed for a hundred years. The radical Micklem challenged the established ways, bringing two novel attributes to the discussion: a social conscience and a keen business mind.

Representative teams were selected from chaps of good family and the swankier public schools. Gerald wanted the best golfers and brought in working-class players, covertly buying Ronnie Shade a dinner jacket to dampen the shock waves agitating the reactionaries.

The Open Championship was in serious decline. Gerald revitalized it and set it on a business-like footing so that profits could be reinvested into even better championships which attracted all the world's best.

The rules were a legalistic hotchpotch fully understood only by a handful of specialists. Gerald initiated the continuing process of rationalizing and reviewing them and wrote a booklet, 'Help in the Interpretation of the Rules', which has become a standard work for the bewildered.

He himself would disclaim personal responsibility for those achievements, pointing out that the game was run by committees of which he was one member, but everyone knew that he supplied the ideas and provided the irresistible dynamic which quelled all opposition.

For these reforms he was awarded the CBE, an inadequate reward in the view of those who understood the magnitude of his contribution, but those were possibly the least of his legacies.

Privately, he became a major patron, always concealing his generosity by stealth, which makes it impossible to quantify the amount of good he spread about within the game. But there can be few worthy young amateurs during his time who were not helped, directly or indirectly, by his conviction that poverty should not disqualify a youngster from competing in amateur golf. Ironically, his official status meant that he had to defend and uphold the rigid rules of amateur status in public while privately he dissipated his fortune in breach of it.

There can have been few more avid spectators of golf than Gerald. Until he was grounded by a debilitating illness, he devoted the major part of his time to travelling to championships, amateur and professional, and tirelessly walking the course, always with a purpose. He wanted to see how Green would tackle a stretch of holes, whether a tendency to hook under pressure would betray Brown at the water hole, whether Black's new grip was bedding down.

Life will never be the same again without the oracle to whom we could turn for the definitive word on the great issues of golf.

(OBSERVER 1988)

Remembering Longhurst

Looking back on his brief foray into parliamentary life, Henry Longhurst wrote: 'It was on the assumption of an electorate consisting of reasonable men that I ventured into politics. Oh, dear. Oh, dear.'

Anyone who loves golf, and that must add up to a world-wide constituency of at least 30 million people, must be grateful that the voters of Acton gave Henry the heave-ho in Britain's postwar Socialist landslide.

Not that Longhurst was a bad MP. On the contrary, he was a dedicated and effective guardian of the rights of the people of Acton. In due course, he would surely have been promoted, and he would have made a disastrous Minister since his political views were those of a feudal baron. Besides, and this is the point, the world would have lost a sublime writer and broadcaster on the game of golf.

From the moment I was appointed as golf correspondent to a newspaper in direct opposition to his, Henry always addressed me jocularly as Hated Rival, and the first words he spoke to me were typical of the man. A pushy public relations officer had been pestering us to go and look at a Caribbean golf development and Henry said, 'I would not presume to offer you any advice on how to go about this job of golf writing except in this one respect. By all means screw their women and drink their booze, but never, never, on any account, write one word about their bloody awful golf courses.'

The formative influences on Longhurst are all too easy to trace. From his comfortable middle-class home in Bedford, where his family had a retail house-furnishing business, Henry was sent to a prep school at Eastbourne, which was to become the subject of some of the most vitriolic prose in the English language by his literary contemporaries.

Henry recalled the morning dish of cold breakfast porridge, into which he once actually threw up. He was then forced to stand in the corner until he had consumed the vile mess – despite which, in his autobiography, *My Life and Soft Times*, he remembered the place with affection, quoting with approval a letter he received many years later: 'My brother attributes the fact that he emerged absolutely sane and fit from five years as a prisoner of war solely to having been at St Cyprians.'

Charterhouse, with its private slang and individual rituals (including a peculiarly barbarous form of corporal punishment) common to all English public schools, gave Longhurst its unmistakable imprint and passed him onto Clare College, Cambridge, where he remained spiritually for the rest of his life.

It is a curious aspect of British university life that while Oxford men emerge with no permanent taint, Cambridge imparts a certain hauteur and plummy smugness, evident in attitude and speech, which brands its alumni for life. That, at least, was the case when the universities were concerned to prepare undergraduates for life, and Longhurst was recognizable as a Cambridge man at a hundred yards until the day he died.

He studied golf, and dabbled in economics in odd moments of his spare time with no great distinction. Golf opened up a whole world for Longhurst. Travelling about the country with the Cambridge team for matches against different clubs, he gained an entrée into the golfing branch of the old boy network which opened the door for his career.

The golfing Mafia spoke the right words into the right ears, and Longhurst was invited to join the *Sunday Times, Tatler* and the London *Evening Standard*.

If Longhurst received a helpful push in the right direction, he quickly proved that he was the right man for the job. He always claimed the status of gifted amateur, since he knew nothing and cared less about the nuts and bolts of journalism, but really he was the most painstaking of professionals. Bernard Darwin had emancipated the golf writer, and Longhurst extended the process. He studied the prose styles of Winston Churchill and P. G. Wodehouse, learning from both the value of economy and simplicity. In twenty-one years, he never missed his weekly column and for thousands of us that essay was an essential ingredient of Sunday breakfast.

Writers who choose to specialize in sport can seldom hope to receive due recognition from the literary fraternity, mainly because the limp-wristed coterie of critics who arbitrate on such matters does not approve of the subject. In fact, one of Longhurst's secrets was that he did not write very much about golf. He took golf as a text and then frequently digressed into some subject which had taken his interest, and he was a man with an insatiable curiosity.

His motto might well have been 'Try Anything Once', and this thirst for new experiences led him to try his hand at motor racing on the old Brooklands track, bobsledding down the Cresta run, going up in a glider, sinking deep into the sea in a diver's suit and riding on the footplate of a locomotive.

Golf enabled him to travel widely and he made the most of his opportunities, always anxious to divert from the beaten path and see new things, do new things. It was a rich life, and vastly enriching for his readers, and Longhurst accumulated a huge repertory of anecdotes, many of them of a disreputable nature, which made him the most wonderful talker I have ever met. I once sat up all night while Longhurst and Alistair Cooke swapped stories. It was like a tennis match as they capped each other's offerings for hour after hour while I poured the gin and listened.

This gift of storytelling lay at the heart of Longhurst's success as a broadcaster. He pioneered golf commentating on radio and television, and set a standard no one has remotely approached since. He seemed to have an instinct for knowing when not to speak on TV and letting the pictures tell their own story. And when he did comment, dismissing a missed putt with an urbane growl of 'Ah, well, *there* we are, then,' it was twenty times more effective than the effusions of hysterical and misinformed rubbish most commentators inflict on the viewer.

Longhurst cheerfully admitted to being a bit of a snob. He rationalized his preference for dukes to dustmen by saying that they were invariably more interesting, and it was this element of snobbery, I believe, which made him slightly uneasy at being branded a journalist, a profession which carries a powerful social stigma in certain quarters, notably in the world of golf.

He was fond of telling the story of attending a championship at a Yorkshire club in his early days when a potting shed was considered quite adequate as working quarters for the despised press. A senior writer had protested at these arrangements, and Longhurst happened to be busily writing in the shed when the secretary and a committeeman passed by and he heard one of them say, 'There's one of them in there now.'

That disdainful remark has passed into the vocabulary of golf writers and is used to this day whenever the press is disparaged. Longhurst delighted in deflating that kind of pomposity, but at the same time he kept himself slightly aloof from the journalistic pack.

In many ways Longhurst led the most enviable of lives, and he knew it. He lost no opportunity to gloat to his readers about being in some exotic place, lazing, with only the clink of ice against glass to disturb the perfect peace. As I know all too well, following the golf trail is not all beer and skittles, and Longhurst also suffered private tragedies which must have made the cheerful tone of his writing excessively difficult to sustain.

Both his son and son-in-law were killed in wasteful accidents. He himself suffered horribly with illness, and was brought to the brink of suicide. He wrote in his column about that incident, revealing that he overdid the job of fortifying his nerves and fell asleep before he could swallow the tablets.

Later, after a good recovery, I asked him about his health. 'I have to go back every three months for a checkup,' he said. 'I always ask for the last appointment of the day so that if the prognosis is unfavourable the pubs will be open.'

Finally, the prognosis was unfavourable. I do hope Henry's glass was full. He would not like to go out on a wave of sentiment and sorrow. Let us remember his zest and wit, and what better way than with a snatch of Longhurst prose, written in his beloved windmill home on the Sussex Downs for his autobiography:

> Bobby [his bull terrier] had a wooden pole, five feet long and the best part of three inches thick, which must have weighed several pounds. It was his great delight to get this pole by the point of balance in his massive jaws and run flat out with it, straight at an opening in the wall about three feet wide. The collision was frightful to behold and sometimes he would somersault clean over the pole at impact. With blood coming from his back teeth he would then collect the pole, retire and charge again.

Henry Longhurst was a bit like that with some of his opinions. The world is a poorer, duller place without him.

The master on the master.

(GOLF WORLD 1978)

TWO: RULES AND CLUB GOLF

When is a 'drop' allowed?

Three good habits to speed play

My first instinct was to curse Jack Nicklaus for ruining a perfectly good theory. Picture the scene. Hours of research, delving into records and turning up references, followed by the obligatory period of staring at the wall while this mass of statistical information churned in the mind like dirty laundry clanking away in the washing machine. Then, the spin-dry cycle, followed by holding each garment up to the light for stains. No, the theory seemed to be without blemish, namely that people who played golf excessively slow were doomed to short careers.

Then I examined Jack Nicklaus, one of the more deliberate golfers of the age and still going strong after a quarter of a century. More gazing at the wallpaper. It gradually dawns that Jack Nicklaus has blown holes in every theory and truism in the game. Swing the clubhead; Nicklaus gives the ball a powerful hit. Turn the shoulders; Nicklaus has a pronounced tilt. Jack of all trades, master of none; Nicklaus is a master of at least four trades: golfer, architect, business administrator and promoter. Therefore, if a theory is to have any validity, Jack Nicklaus must be the exception that proves the rule. All was not lost.

The idea that slow play means a short golf life is not claimed as an original discovery. The good Douglas Michael Fortunato, or Doug Ford as he is sometimes known, was preaching this doctrine twenty years ago, and he was not the first by any means. Ford insisted that taking too much time over a golf shot cut short the life of a tournament professional and could in all likelihood add quite a number of strokes to the scores of all golfers.

Slow play and excessive concentration took so much out of a man that he could not play too often or for too long. Ford cited the example of Dr Cary Middlecoff, who was notorious for the time and intensity he expended over every stroke, and forecast that he would burn himself out prematurely. Shortly afterward, Middlecoff retired from competitive golf.

Byron Nelson was not slow, but he exhausted his resources of nervous energy with every round, like Bobby Jones. Both retired early because they could not continue. Mostly, the furious concentration of mental effort is accompanied by a dilatory progress, as in the case of the young David Graham. In 1972, at the Australian Open, he was given a hard time by officials over the slowness of his play. I asked Graham if he did not feel a responsibility to the people who had paid to watch him, and he was adamant in his denial. As a professional his first responsibility was to produce his best golf and he would take as much time as he felt was needed. As Graham matured he played more briskly and better.

In the 1955 US Open played at the Olympic Club in San Francisco, the players went out in groups of three and took an average of 4 hours 27 minutes to play the first round. In the final round, playing in twos, the average was 3 hours 13 minutes. Ten years later, these times had increased by exactly an hour in both cases. The round of five-hours-plus has been with us ever since and the malaise has spread through every level of the game.

For tournament professionals, this excessive amount of time to complete a round is not something they necessarily need or want. It has become a habit that is preferable to playing at a reasonable pace and then having to wait ten minutes or more on the next tee, with muscles growing stiff, until the fairway is clear.

To have slow-play marshals on the course chivying groups at random merely creates bad blood because golf is like a convoy, its speed dictated by the pace of the slowest ship. The same criticism applies to fixing the maximum timescales for the play of an individual stroke and then having observers crouching behind bushes with stopwatches at the ready.

The only effective way is to determine a reasonable amount of time for the round to be completed and then to monitor the progress of the first group of the day, applying the appropriate penalties to them and to all the following groups that allow one clear hole to open up ahead of them.

A few victims might squeal, but I am sure that the general body of pro golf would quickly adjust to an accelerated pace and would revive good playing habits without detriment to their scores. These good habits are well enough known but since there are only three it will not waste much space to repeat them for the record:

1. Assess your shot while others are playing so that you will be ready to fire when it is your turn.

2. Cultivate a fixed routine so that when your turn comes you can go through an automatic progression of selecting a club, making a practice swing, addressing the ball and swinging. That way, as Ford suggests, you do not have a chance to second-guess yourself.

3. Walk briskly between shots. If the pros were allowed to demonstrate these virtues, then the rest of golf would soon follow suit, although I doubt whether anyone could ever emulate the feat of the late Henry Howell, Welsh amateur and international player, and member of the Glamorganshire Golf Club.

Henry went to the club after work on the last qualifying day for a match-play competition. He had not turned in a medal card to qualify for the competition proper and by now there was not enough daylight left to get in eighteen holes, as one of the members pointed out. Here was a challenge, and to Henry that suggested an opportunity. 'You want to bet?' he inquired. The first offer was that he could not score 72 in an hour and a half. Henry accepted and raised the odds. The bets came thick and fast, the most extreme being that he could not go round in 67 in an hour and a quarter. A marker, a timekeeper, a caddie and a referee were appointed, and off they went with a gallery of confident gamblers.

The last putt dropped precisely 68 minutes later and Henry had gone round in 32–31 = 63.

To put it mildly, that must have been a thoroughly enjoyable round of golf, to play and to watch. It is not enjoyable to play slowly and it is positively disagreeable to be forced to play slowly because of a dilatory group in front. And, after all, the whole purpose of golf is to enjoy it.

(Golf Digest 1987)

Wimps of the world unite

Sadly for golf, a high proportion of new developments are new-money projects. With the Cayman Islands in danger of sinking under the new weight of his newly acquired wealth, the self-made squillionaire succumbs to golf fever. Once he has built his dream home with sunken marble baths and gold fittings, Andy Warhol originals, libraries of leather-bound books bought by the yard and other expressions of bad taste, he turns his attention to golf.

He buys a tract of land. As a businessman he would never dream of commissioning a champion riveter to design a battle-ship, but golf makes us all irrational. So, he sends for a famous professional golfer to design the course.

The famous professional golfer makes enthusiastic notes about the potential of the site and returns to base. He goes down to the basement where serried ranks of real golf course architects are toiling at their drawing boards. He briefs the supervisor.

'This clown wants a championship course.'

The supervisor makes a note: '7,500 yards'.

'It has to be challenging.'

The supervisor writes: 'Lots of water'.

'And spectacular.'

The supervisor scribbles: 'Fountains, flower beds, rockeries, *ad nauseam*'. He enquires, 'Are we doing the clubhouse as well?'

'Oh, sure. I forgot that. Give it the full works.'

'Well, we have the plans for a full-scale replica of the Palace

Versailles faced with coloured glass cladding. It was left over from that project in Japan that went belly-up.'

'Sounds good. Go to it.'

In due course, the client sends out lavish brochures, richly illustrated by coloured photographs of the course and clubhouse. The text is spattered with copywriter's jargon, such as 'space age technology' and 'state of the art'. The cost of every element of the development is given due prominence as a guarantee of quality.

All of the above is absolutely fine by me. Strain as I might, I am unable to detect the faintest detail calling for criticism or complaint.

But the brochures are all too often accompanied by a gushing invitation to join a galaxy of stars of stage, sport and politics for the grand opening of this new, exclusive, no-expense-spared masterpiece. A stamped postcard is enclosed to confirm my attendance along with a map, a request for my handicap and a reminder to bring my clubs.

Over the welcoming coffee, we guests are addressed by the founder, the architect, a civic dignitary and the greenkeeper. Hostesses hired from an agency hand out sleeves of logoed golf balls, logoed towels, a logoed pack of tees (which we stuff in our pockets) and massive folders containing reams of information, from the membership financial structure down to the type of fertilizer used on the Pennpiffle 487 greens (which we leave on our chairs).

Then, a public relations official, crackling with forced bonhomie, announces the programme for the day, including the form of play. He invariably concludes with the chilling announcement: 'We know that you will want to experience the real golf course so we are putting you off the back tees.'

There, in one sentence, he destroys all the good work performed by a promotional budget equivalent to the gross national product of Paraguay.

Six hours later, the first group trudges back to the clubhouse with the weary, shell-shocked air of survivors returning from the Hundred Years' War. Those three new balls now rest at the bottom of the lake which creates the 220-yard carry at the first short hole. The human wreckage slumps onto the locker room benches. Every man has a grisly tale to tell of the double-figures incurred at the 'feature hole', or of the clubs smashed at the seventeenth while trying to extricate his ball from the boulders shipped in from Phoenix or handcrafted in cement because it looks more natural.

To a man they swear that nothing will persuade them ever to set foot again on this godawful abortion of a golf course. But if only that grinning lout had put us off the middle tees, we would have been bursting with gratitude and praising the course to the heavens. For 18-handicappers, the average stand-ard of such gatherings, the real golf course is one played from the forward men's tees.

Unfortunately, it is not only bone-headed PR people who have this fixation about the real course being the version played from the championship tees. I have often played classic courses with friends who are otherwise quite sensible, yet every time one of them has proposed: 'Why don't we play it off the back like the pros?' And the other three of us, fearful of being branded as wimps, have fallen in with this cretinous suggestion and had a thoroughly lousy day because of it.

Never again. Golf, as I frequently remark, should be a pleasure, not a penance. Regardless of handicap strokes, the pleasure of golf can only be obtained by playing from the tee markers appropriate to your standard of skill. Let us demand our rights. Wimps of the world unite. Forward to the middle tees!

(GOLF WORLD 1992)

A phrase for all reasons

Attention, please. Is there a young man or woman in the audience with an enquiring mind, independent means and access to a good golf library? I have a challenging research project which could well occupy a lifetime. It is to identify the person who started the convention of saying 'Good shot' every time an opponent or fellow competitor hits one flush off the screws.

So far as the professionals are concerned, I think we can narrow down the search area to this century, for it is difficult to imagine Andra Kirkaldy growling compliments to J. H. Taylor. Indeed, Ben Hogan never indulged in such insincerities, uttering not a single word on one famous occasion when his companion holed-in-one.

As for the amateurs, the researcher who casts his net must trawl through half a millennium in search of the culprit. It is all too easy to imagine some lickspittle courtier gushing 'Well smitten, sire' every time King James made contact with the ball.

Whoever the 'Good shot' pioneer might have been I want to know because I intend to pin his picture on my dartboard. The words 'Good shot' pierce me like a dagger through the heart and I want that ratbag to taste some of his own medicine.

Why, you may wonder, should a common courtesy get so far up this fellow Dobereiner's nose? Well, take those words 'Good shot'. According to circumstances, 'good' may mean good, lucky (for him), lucky (for you), indifferent, surprising, bad, timely or absolutely nothing at all. Professionals, who are innately honest folk, do not bother with such a capricious word and simply say 'Shot', a reflex response which carries about twenty-seven meanings, the main one being: 'Note what jolly good sportsmen we professionals are, to be sure.'

The first 'Good shot' is commonly uttered in encouraging tones by a teaching pro or parent and expresses the sentiment, 'At last after a hundred exhortations this uncoordinated dummy has got it through his thick skull that you have to hit down to get the ball up. Thank goodness for that; I was beginning to fear he must be retarded.'

From then on, 'Good shot' becomes part of the routine litany of the game. Some golfers become proficient enough to earn regular salutations of 'Good SHOT!' when the words, for once, mean what they say and are sincerely meant. In a long golfing life I only once qualified for a 'Good SHOT!' and there was no one there to utter it.

It was very early in the morning and the course was enveloped in a thick ground mist which extended about waist high. I could see the top half of the flagstick and took a careful bearing on it as I strode into the dense forest of beech trees to locate my drive. The ball was lying well but chipping out was not an option; I could spend the day clattering about among the tree trunks. Then, I noticed a small patch of blue sky in the canopy and, glory be, I calculated it was bang in line with my target.

The shot, meticulously planned for elevation and direction, was perfectly executed. The ball rose like an arrow and sped through that tiny gap high among the tree tops. I dashed out of the wood and emerged just in time to see the ball plummeting down dead on target.

You can imagine my elation as I hurried forward, just as you can imagine my feelings on finding the ball sitting six inches from a rake which had been stuck into a fairway bunker a hundred yards short of the green. Even so, it was a genuine candidate for a 'Good SHOT!'

With advancing years and declining powers, the ritual

'Good shot' begins to sound a jarring note. After spending most of my working life watching the finest exponents of the game, I ought to be able to recognize a good shot when I see one. Getting the ball close to the target does not by any means automatically constitute a good shot. It becomes mildly irksome to be complimented when a squirty one off the toe happens to find a good result.

But worse is to come. In the sere and yellow years, 'Good shot' is invariably spoken with a rising inflexion which betrays astonishment rather than admiration. The words lacerate my soul. My companions might just as well come right out with it and express their true feelings: 'Well, who would have guessed that the old dodderer could suddenly pull one of those out of the bag? Wonders will never cease.'

There is only one valid reason for saying 'Good shot' and that is for purposes of gamesmanship. If you have a good ear you can tell at the moment of impact when your opponent catches the ball slightly off the snout. If you say 'Good shot' and keep any hint of sarcasm out of your voice, then you have got him.

He knows he has hit a bad one and asks himself: 'Does this clown really think that was one of my good ones?' Now you reinforce your reputation for sportsmanship by shouting 'Hook! Hook!' at his ball until it clatters among the trees on the right. You kill him off by remarking solicitously, 'Damn wind got it. Tough.' His money is in your pocket.

(GOLF WORLD 1992)

What is a stroke?

Since golf is a game in which the winner is the player who takes the fewest number of strokes, it is important that we all understand exactly what is meant by a stroke.

SMART ALEC: For goodness sake! Everybody knows what a stroke is. It's when you hit the ball.

DEVIL'S ADVOCATE: What if you miss the ball?

S.A.: That's a whiff, or air shot, and that's a stroke, too.

D.A.: But a practice swing is not a stroke.

S.A.: No, because in that case you are not trying to hit the ball. There has to be an *intention*. Let me read you the official definition: 'A stroke is the forward movement of the club made with the intention of fairly striking at and moving the ball.'

D.A.: I see. So, the stroke does not begin until the club starts to move forward?

S.A.: Exactly. That's why you can stop and start again if you are disturbed at the top of your backswing.

D.A.: Wait a minute. There are two forward movements of the club during the swing. As you complete the backswing the club is moving forward toward the target. Then it moves backward, away from the target, at the start of the downswing. It does not move forward again until the hands are hip-high on the downswing. So, where does the stroke begin?

S.A.: It is generally accepted that the stroke starts with the beginning of the downswing.

D.A.: So when the definition says 'forward' it really means to say: 'The precise moment when the club has ceased to move forward and is about to move backward for the second time since the address position?'

S.A.: You're nit-picking, but that's about the size of it. Anyway, what does it matter?

D.A.: Well, it matters for two reasons. First, the USGA insists that in the rules every word means what it says. Now, if the USGA means what it says when it says that every word means what it says, then it is unfortunate that it uses the word 'forward' when it means 'backward', or possibly 'downward'. Second, it is critical to establish exactly when a stroke begins. As you know, if a ball falls off its tee before a stroke is made, it can be re-teed without penalty. But if a stroke is made in such circumstances, then that stroke must count.

S.A.: In that case, we must accept that a stroke has been made once the downswing has begun.

D.A.: Right. It would be wildly impractical to try to measure the moment when the club starts moving forward halfway through the downswing. But in a recent case a player saw his ball topple off the tee just as he was starting to move his club backward – or forward as the USGA describes it.

S.A.: So the stroke had to count.

D.A.: Not at all. The player claimed that he aborted his intention to strike the ball as soon as he saw it fall, therefore it was not a stroke within the meaning of the rules. The USGA upheld his claim and published a Decision to that effect.

S.A.: Is that true?

D.A.: Absolutely. I swear it.

S.A.: But even if he moved the club only one-hundredth of an inch forward – or backward if you are going to be pedantic – and then aborted his intention, he still had made a stroke. After all, his intention was there during that hundredth of an inch. We all have that intention right from the instant we start the takeaway.

D.A.: I could not have put it better myself.

S.A.: But that Decision makes nonsense of the definition of a stroke.

D.A.: The definition was nonsensical anyway. We have been through all that.

S.A.: Still, that Decision has all the force of a Rule of Golf. I am beginning to get an idea.

D.A.: Tell me more.

S.A.: Well, like most high-handicap players, I have a pretty good idea that the stroke has gone haywire even before the clubface meets the ball. I get that Oh-my-God-I've-come-across-it feeling.

D.A.: Me, too. Indeed, I've incorporated a shout of 'Fore!' in my backswing, plus a yell of 'Oh, Hell!' as an integral part of my follow-through.

S.A.: But according to this Decision, I can abort my stroke as soon as I feel that I'm coming into the ball all wrong.

D.A.: So it would appear.

S.A.: And then, when I snap one into the water hazard, I can claim that I had not made a stroke.

D.A.: Always provided that you honestly did abort your intention before the club met the ball.

S.A.: Of course. It must be an honest abortion. Still, in such a case I would be perfectly entitled to play the shot over again.

D.A.: Over and over again until you hit one straight. That is the clear implication of the Decision.

S.A.: And then I could go on aborting my approach shots until I hit one close to the pin.

D.A.: A rule is a rule. You are entitled to use it to your advantage.

S.A.: Do you suppose I could abort the odd putt?

D.A.: Why not? It is a stroke within the definition. In fact, it is the only stroke within the definition, since it does start with a forward movement.

S.A.: If I aborted enough bad shots, I could go around in 65 every time.

D.A.: Only if you were playing in a competition where you could be sure that the officials knew the rules and were prepared to administer them fairly and without prejudice.

SMART ALEC: You mean the US Open. You're right. I'll go out and win the Open.

DEVIL'S ADVOCATE: And the best of luck to you, sir.

One of Peter's favourite pet peeves: the phrasing of the Rules of Golf. *They gave him, and his readers, endless hours of amusement.*

(GOLF DIGEST 1979)

b.

The true definitions of golf

It has been sagely established by George Bernard Shaw, unless perchance it may have been some other witty blighter such as Oscar Wilde or Noel Coward, that the invention of private languages, as practised by all the learned professions, constitutes a conspiracy against the public. If the law was written in plain English, all lawyers would starve.

Golf is guilty of the same con trick, so for the benefit of the uninitiated I offer a glossary of some common golf terms.

Anti-trust law: Powerful nerve gas, one whiff of which induces complete loss of marbles in the guardians of golf's standards and equipment, causing them to hide in a broom cupboard and sing 'Anything Goes' in a hysterical falsetto.

Broomstick: Golf club.

Final (as in 'the referee's decision is final'): Interim, tentative, hypothetical. If you don't like his ruling, you can tell him to go ... whatever.

Forbidden: Permitted, as in 'the committee has no power to waive a Rule of Golf', except that the committees of the pro tours waive and modify rules and regulations until the game is barely recognizable.

Forwards: Backwards, as in the definition of a stroke: 'A forward movement of the club, etc.' when it really means the first movement from the top of the backswing which is, of course, backwards.

Green (as in 'through the green'): All the cultivated areas of the hole being played except the green. See **Through**.

Immovable obstruction: Mobile crane capable of speeds of up to 80 mph (US Open Championship, Oakmont, 1994).

Inside: Outside, and vice versa, in case of taking relief from an immovable obstruction in a hazard. The rules insist you drop both inside and outside the hazard.

Moving: Stationary, as in the case of a ball firmly wedged in the branch of a tree which is waving wildly in the wind. See **Stationary**.

Not permitted (as in 'appendages to the main body of the head ... are not permitted'. Appendix 11, *Rules of Golf*): Permitted by all means, especially in the case of driver heads shaped like branding irons and fancy, plastic balls adorning Dave Pelz putters.

Ocean: This word is used in two senses in *Rules of Golf*, with a distinct but almost undetectably subtle difference in meaning according to context. It might mean either: 1. a water hazard (Defintion 42), or, 2. definitely and absolutely not a water hazard. Really. What sort of person would try to pull a devious stunt like calling an ocean a water hazard (Decision 26–1/7)?

Open: Shut. At the address, when the toe of the club is inclined to the right, or rotated in a clockwise direction, it is said to be 'open' but when similarly inclined, or rotated in a clockwise direction, at the top of the backswing it is said to be 'shut'. When used in the context of competitions, such as the Open Championship, the adjective 'open' means severely restricted to less than one hundredth part of 1 per cent of the golfing population, or virtually hermetically sealed.

Plain (as in 'the clubhead shall be generally plain in shape'. Appendix 11, *Rules of Golf*): As fancy and convoluted as the diseased imagination of a club designer can devise.

Retail: The manufacturing cost of golf equipment multiplied by 100.

Royal and Ancient Golf Club: Ruling body for golf in parts of the world not administered by the US Golf Association. The R&A does not conspire (heaven forbid) or confer (perish the thought) with the USGA in making rules, regulations and decisions covering golf equipment (see **Anti-trust law**), yet the two authorities magically contrive to produce identical legislation, presumably by means of extrasensory perception.

Stationary: Moving. When a ball is teetering on the lip of the cup but still clearly in motion, or when accelerating at 32 feet per second as it disappears over Niagara Falls, the Rules insist it is perfectly immobile, permitting you to take a whack at it with impunity. See **Moving**.

Through (as in 'through the green'): Throughout.

Traditional (as in 'traditional form and make' in definition of a golf club): Surrealist abomination invented yesterday and manufactured in Taiwan.

Wood: Any metal, resin or ceramic, provided it is not remotely associated with trees, as may be used for the manufacture of woods. In the plural, i.e. Tiger Woods, the word means a perfect opportunity for Americans to demonstrate their broadminded, integrated, enlightened, PC attitudes by lavishing extravagant praise on a promising young golfer during discussions in the bar of their all-white golf clubs. Also, groups of trees into which the new, long-shafted, big-headed and patently non-conforming (see **Anti-trust law**) drivers despatch the ball further and deeper.

World tour: A good, if obvious, idea which would be of inestimable benefit to the game of golf and to the players. It therefore finds small favour with the men who run the American and European tours.

Another example of Peter's pre-occupation with the absurdities of the rulebook.

(GOLF WORLD 1995)

THREE: COURSES AND COUNTRIES

The magic of Ireland.

The magic of Ireland

I worry about Ireland. Every time I go there I am like a puppy having its first encounter with a hedgehog. The experience is at once fascinating and perplexing and frustrating. You cannot move in Ireland without running your nose onto the sharp spike of paradox.

The saddest paradox is still to come. The country's main asset is its haunting and timeless beauty. And in order to survive, Ireland must attract tourists in such numbers as to destroy the very quality that makes it attractive. Who wants to visit a silent valley echoing with the blare of motor horns? Or march across a Connemara bespattered with caravans?

The Irish know it is happening, and they recoil from the prospect of their land becoming no more than a view from a hotel window and themselves picturesque figures to animate this landscape. They know they are eating their seed corn. Except in this case, being Irish, they are distilling it into their peculiar brand of anaesthetic. As a result, they live in a mood of haphazard gusto and strictly day to day.

When I go to Ireland, I normally order a hire car in advance, so that it is waiting for me on arrival. In theory, that is. In practice, I have lost count of the number of times I have been told, 'Sorry, sir, we have no reservation in that name.' On the other hand, whenever this has happened, I have invariably and without compunction been given a car reserved for someone else.

Experiences like this are inescapable. The Irish like to tell the story of the German industrialist who set up a factory in

Ireland. He set out with Teutonic efficiency to establish his business, and was soon at the brink of insanity. Whenever there was a wedding or a funeral or a coming-of-age party in the neighbourhood, the entire factory staff simply took the day off, mostly being distantly related to each other and joined by an even stronger bond if they weren't: free booze is thicker than blood.

Faced with the choice of losing his mind, or his factory, or both, the German sensibly decided that if he couldn't beat them he must join them. He became an Irishman by association, a sort of honorary second cousin, and joined in the festivities at every opportunity. He went to all the wakes and cried and drank and called for another chorus of 'Molly Malone und her veelbarrow mit'. And the odd thing was that, despite all the unscheduled stoppages, the productivity per head was higher than in any of his other factories in Europe.

There must be a moral there somewhere. About four times a year, my golfing work requires me to visit Ireland, and on every occasion, as the date approaches, the prospect produces an irrational excitement. Part of it is a foreboding amounting to a racing certainty that such plans as I have been foolish enough to make are going to be irreparably wrecked. Partly it is the realization that many of the most memorable experiences in my life have been in the company of Irishmen – and many of the near-disasters, for that matter, in the company of Irish women.

Before each trip I give myself a lecture. Ireland is a fully paid-up member of the twentieth-century community of nations. Its technology is as advanced as anybody's. I tell myself firmly that Ireland is no different from any other civilized country. All that Pat and Mick rubbish is just the comic patter of professional entertainers and has absolutely no relevance to contemporary Ireland.

Thus, freed of all preconceived misconceptions about the place, I arrive, briefcase in hand, ready to do business. And so it is that I am always caught off balance by the sheer Irishness of the place.

It happens suddenly. Once, within fifteen minutes of landing, I was driving into the interior with my resistance getting lower by the minute from the bliss of driving on roads virtually free of other traffic. Thanks to what I take to be a national pastime of breaking off signposts so that only a stump remains containing one or two letters, I became lost. Nothing unusual in that.

The only living creatures I could see were an elderly man and a pig. The man was standing in the middle of the road and trying to stuff the struggling creature into a sack. (Don't ask me – I haven't the slightest idea.) I asked if he could direct me. 'Let me see, now,' he said, repeating my destination two or three times. 'Lisburn ... Lisburn, now.' He screwed his face into a frenzy of concentration. At last, he seemed to get it straight in his mind and drew a deep breath in preparation for what were obviously going to be pretty complicated instructions. He fixed me with a look which implied that if I hoped to grasp the Theory of Relativity in one gulp, I'd better keep my wits about me. I responded with due attention.

'You carry along on this road.'

'Along this road.'

'And then you come to a town.'

'A town. Got it.'

'And when you get into the town, you turn ...'

'Yes?'

'Nowhere!'

And so it was. Absolutely straight ahead. For a while, I turned over the theory that he was a plant, paid by the Irish Tourist Board to give local colour to susceptible visitors. But it happens too often.

The same day another stranger directed me to carry on until I came to a fork and then go straight ahead. You'd need an army of unemployed actors to work such a scheme. It has to be genuine.

Irishness flourishes in many forms. No doubt it still drives creative men like Shaw to emigrate in gloomy frustration. In small, well-rationed doses I find it engaging.

You may be wondering what all this has to do with golf. It is simply this: whereas Irishness can be tiresome in the extreme to a visiting dynamic businessman anxious to get on with the job, it is perfectly attuned to golf. The game is leisurely, paradoxical and depends for enjoyment on social contact. So is Ireland. It is a perfect mix. The people, the climate and the lifestyle all conspire to improve the golf and give it a unique flavour.

At this point a small personal confession is necessary. When the Irish talk about their own whimsicalities it may be mawkish but at least they have every right to pull their own legs. For a foreigner to do so can all too easily sound patronizing or superior. I am aware of the danger and so must quickly point out that when it comes to what the efficiency experts call Organization and Method, I am a complete non-starter.

The clerks in the booking office of my local railway station are no longer surprised when I put a pound on the counter and ask for a packet of cigarettes. And, like others before me, I have been known, on arrival in London in my Sunday-go-to-meeting suit, to telephone home to ask where I am supposed to be going. So, if I make gentle fun of Ireland I can assure you that Ireland, in the form of my many friends there, takes ample and justified revenge.

With that preamble out of the way I can progress with my story, which began with a kindly editor ordering me to go and play a round at Portmarnock with Harry Bradshaw. I had two projected trips to Ireland coming up, the first to Belfast and then later to Dublin. Obviously, it would be much more convenient to visit Portmarnock while I was in the neighbourhood on the Dublin visit.

Needless to say, when I got to Belfast I telephoned Harry and said that I believed we were supposed to play golf, and how about Thursday. It says much for him that not by so much as a tremor in his voice did he betray any surprise at a lunatic calling him up to keep an appointment six weeks early. 'Sure, that will be grand,' he said. It was months later that I discovered that I'd got it all wrong.

Those who have never seen The Brad hit a golf ball have missed a unique experience. The Irish do not take kindly to regimentation. They are too individualistic. So, while the English and Scots, and to a large extent the Americans, work to mould their golf into a classic style, the Irish pay little attention to correctness of form. They are not concerned with how they look so much as how they score, and while it is true that they do not have correct golf coached into them, it is equally true that they don't have natural ability coached out of them.

As a result, most of the Irish professionals have 'faulty' techniques. Christy O'Connor commits the cardinal sin of flicking at the ball instead of keeping arms and club in one solid entity through the ball. Wristy Christy has never lost a moment's sleep over this fault from the time he became the first man to win a four-figure cheque on the British circuit to the time he won a record £31,532 in the 1970 season. Jimmy Kinsella uses a driver with two shafts, one hammered down inside the other, thus putting superfluous weight in all the wrong places. He wields this absurdly unsuitable weapon with an action which led me to describe him as the only man who plays golf without a backswing. His method is a compromise between a convulsion and a lunge. It is a hopeless parody of a golf swing, and the only redeeming feature about it is that he hits the ball farther and straighter than most professionals.

Paddy Skerritt, by comparison, is almost orthodox except in his temperament, which is totally unconventional. Concentration, as we are constantly being reminded by the experts, is half of golf. You can tell that the great players are concentrating by the way they prowl around, scowling and cursing. They toss bits of grass into the air to test the wind, and pace off distances, and ask the galleries to keep quiet, and swear at photographers, and make dozens of practice swings. Skerritt seems to imagine that you can play golf without any of these preliminaries. He never scowls. Even when his ball goes into a bunker he just gives a wry smile and hits it out. Otherwise, he simply looks at the target and makes his shot. Just like that. Dammit, he makes golf look like a game.

But none of them are quite so eccentric as Bradshaw. Possibly someone once told him that it cost two penalty strokes if you raised the club above waist level. (It would be just like the Irish to get confused with the rules of hockey.) Anyway, that's the way he plays it, and his attitude on the course is, if possible, even more casual than Skerritt's.

In appearance, Bradshaw looks like a country butcher, portly and ruddy faced and with a cap pulled in the manner of a guardsman so far over his nose that he has to tilt his head back to see out, peering from under his cheese-cutter. Even when he walks onto the tee and hits off, you do not immediately suspect that here is a vastly accomplished professional golfer. For a start, it all happens so quickly. He stoops to tee his ball, takes one glance up the fairway and it has gone, dispatched with a flick from massive hands, straight but not long enough to suggest that he will give you much trouble.

On that perfect day, hot and with hardly a breath of wind, the first hole at Portmarnock looked easy meat. I felt confident that I could sail my drive way past my opponent's ball. I took out my spoon. I did not want to humiliate a great player whose best years were past. A suspicion of a hook took my ball into the rough. Bradshaw trundled his onto the front of the green. As luck would have it, my ball tucked itself into a bank from which I could only hack it back onto the fairway, and so it was just as well that the pitch finished close to the flag. Harry took one glance at the line of his putt and stroked the ball straight into the hole.

I consoled myself that you can't play against flukes. All you can do is plug away and wait for the luck to change. Harry chatted amiably all the while. We talked about the time when he should have won the Open. It was at Sandwich in 1949 and

Harry's ball, by a million-to-one chance, had rolled right into a broken bottle. Would a referee have allowed him to drop clear?

The question is academic because Bradshaw did not ask for a ruling. He smashed the ball out of the bottle with his wedge, a venerable instrument with a brown, enamelled shaft and the thinnest of grips. It had not brought him fortune at Sandwich, because he had lost the play-off against Bobby Locke, but today it was enchanted. He was getting up and down from everywhere. Eventually it penetrated my thick skull that it was not luck at all. It looked like magic all right, but that superannuated wedge and an even older putter were murdering me.

The greens at Portmarnock are, quite simply, the best in the world and on that day they were superb. Even I holed putts from long distances, but I could not live against this man. From a hundred yards out, he was guaranteed to get down in two. I blushed at the memory of having entertained a hope that with my handicap shots and a bit of luck I might give him a game. A little while previously Harry had been engaged to play a filmed TV match at Portmarnock against the redoubtable Billy Casper. As the day approached, the members were torn between loyalty and the seductive odds offered by the local bookies. Harry was having back trouble. And, even without that disability, he was not as long as he had been in his prime.

Casper, on the other hand, was right at the top of his powers and arguably the most accomplished golfer in the world. One of the members put the agonizing problem to Harry. Of course, they all wanted him to win and they would be out there pulling for him. They honoured and respected him, and wanted him to understand that nothing would ever change that situation, but the time was fast approaching when the serious matter of putting down the bets had to be faced. The ties of friendship and loyalty were placing an intolerable strain on their consciences. 'Don't worry about that at all,' said Harry. 'So far as I am concerned it won't make a scrap of difference if you bet on Casper.' These generous words were as comforting as a papal absolution. 'But,' added Harry, 'I can tell you one thing. I will win.' There are sportsmen from whom such words would be meaningless, nothing more than a braggadocio attempt at self-reassurance. Coming from Bradshaw, the statement meant exactly what it said. And, of course, he did win, much to the profit of the faithful, who duly celebrated in fitting style.

Not that the Irish need much encouragement in such matters. After Bernard Hunt won the inaugural Carroll's tournament, the tiles on the clubhouse roof were popping under the strain of the merry-making. In the early hours of the morning, a policeman arrived to investigate what sounded like a revolution, and the following exchange transpired:

'What's going on here?'

'We're celebrating a famous Irish victory.'

'But Bernard Hunt is English.'

'Ssssssh!'

Although incidents like this enliven the life of a golf correspondent, it is not Irish tournament golf which attracts me to Ireland. Tournaments, after all, are still work, even though they may be spiced with a certain element of novelty. My delight, and it is shared by everyone who has experienced it, is to play golf in Ireland. It is probably the last country in the world which can offer the type of golfing experience which used to be enjoyed by the wealthy and privileged in prewar England and Scotland.

As I have already mentioned, driving a motorcar in Ireland still retains an element of recreation. Motoring is a pleasure rather than a chore, and this in itself is a bonus for the golfer. He can put his clubs into the car and be off, on the whim of the moment.

Unless you happen to choose a fashionable Dublin course on a summer weekend, there is no need for preliminary phone calls or formal letters of introduction from the secretary of your own club. You just arrive, pay a tiny green fee and the course is yours. To those who come from countries where golf clubs treat casual visitors as if they were suffering from infectious and fatal diseases, the mere fact of being made to feel welcome is a refreshing change.

But the real change is the courses themselves. A wealthy and well-connected golfer in London can play some wonderful golf courses, but they are basically of two types, heathland or parkland. Edinburgh is rich in golf, but again the choice is limited to links or parkland. Glasgow is the same. From Dublin, however, you are within half an hour's drive of all manner of golf. There are the majestic championship links of Portmarnock and Royal Dublin. There is dunes golf over the Island, lush parkland at Castle. You can play in the clouds among the mountaintops at Howth. Or, if your legs and lungs aren't up to such exertions, you can stroll over the flat clifftop fairways at Woodbrook. There are thirty clubs in and around Dublin and all of them of a different nature. Not all of them are great courses, or even good ones, mind. But they are different certainly.

My own preference, however, is to get right away from cities whenever possible and to ponder on the larger spiritual issues, such as which is the greatest golf course in all the universe. I have narrowed it down to two: Royal County Down on the east coast and Ballybunion on the west. One day, after many more field trials, I trust, I shall arrive at a firm conclusion.

These two are, of course, big and magnificent links. Killarney is magnificent also. But, at the risk of sounding like a travelogue, I would urge that the itinerant golfer in Ireland should on no account neglect the small and out-of-the-way courses. Some of them are ludicrous, and I remember one, which shall be nameless, where the men who built the greens were clearly working from the plans for tees. All the greens are exactly rectangular, like up-turned cake tins.

Others are gems. If you drive through County Kerry and take the right turning off the coast road down a cart track and then again turn down the right track from the previous track, you will, if you are lucky, discover Dooks. I found it by accident, and since there was no one but sheep to whom I could pay a green fee, I slipped what I considered a suitable offering through the letter box of a hut which does duty as a clubhouse and went out to play. Even at the time, it was a dreamlike experience, playing over the rolling hills and guessing, often wrongly, which hollow would harbour a green. I did not see another human all day.

Not that human contact is unrewarding on Irish golf courses. Quite the contrary, as my friend Mark Wilson discovered. He is, if I may say so, without offence, one of those players to whom half the glory of golf is belting the life out of the ball. And being a powerful man, he can belt it with stunning effect.

He went out to play one evening and engaged a caddie, a bright lad with flaming red hair and a keen interest in his master's golfing welfare. They came to a hole with the tee elevated high on a mountainside. The fairway, hard and fast, sloped away below and the fresh breeze blew directly from behind – exactly the circumstances to quicken the pulse of a belter. Mark caught the ball with one of his Sunday specials, right off the screws.

'Boy!' exclaimed the lad. 'That was some drive.' As they walked down the fairway the caddie kept emitting expressions of astonishment and admiration. 'You certainly gave that one the business, mister.' 'That was a real beauty,' and so on. As they came nearer the ball the lad's chatter became more and more excited. At last, he burst out in excitement, 'You've done it. I've seen them all play this hole – O'Connor and Joe Carr and all them big hitters. They none of them ever got it this far. That must be the world record.' He looked at Mark with hero-worshipping awe and added, 'I never did see the like of that drive all my life.' And for the rest of the round he kept up the reference to that Herculean drive. 'Just give her one like you did back there.' All of which was highly agreeable to Mark's ego, and he tipped the lad liberally when they finished.

Later, Mark was talking to the club secretary in the bar and the conversation went like this:

'Good round?'

'Very pleasant, thank you.'

'Enjoy the course?'

'Very much.'

'Caddie all right?'

'Excellent.'

'Which one did you have?'

'Ginger-haired lad, a boy of excellent judgment.'

'Did you tip him well?'

'Yes, I did actually. Why do you ask?'

'At what hole did he tell you that you'd hit the longest drive he'd ever seen in his life?'

'Twelfth . . . . You mean?'

'Everybody. Never fails. It's pretty hard not to get a long way off that twelfth tee. That boy will be a millionaire before he's twenty.'

Finally, if anything I have written should persuade you to try Irish golf for yourself, please don't all rush at once. That would ruin everything. Pick a companion, or two or three. And take care to choose men whose drinking rate corresponds with your own. Then, sneak across quietly in twos or threes and sample the game as it should be played. As it was in the beginning – world without end (if we are lucky).

If there was one country Peter enjoyed to visit more than any other, it was Ireland – north or south. Although this piece was written close to thirty years ago, it still captures perfectly Peter's love and zest for Ireland and the Irish.

(THE GOLFER'S BEDSIDE BOOK 1971)

No place for mugs

N ot to put too fine a point on it, Carnoustie is a pretty good place to emigrate *from*. The little township on the east coast of Scotland, which is to be host to this year's [1975] British Open Championship, has few pretensions to charm. It is just a few streets, with the little stone houses huddled together for warmth, straggling along the railway line from Edinburgh to Aberdeen. By some freak of geography this stretch of coast has its own peculiar climate. Most people who know Carnoustie only from reading about its past Opens have the idea that the place is continuously lashed by gales and/or stinging rain. That is not quite fair. It can be calm here but then, even in mid-summer, it is liable to be visited by a phenomenon known locally as 'haaaaar'. Purists of the Scottish dialect may complain that there are one or two surplus 'a's in that render-ing, but that is the phonetic form of the word, a teeth-chattering exclamation to describe the sea mist which strikes icy daggers into your very bones, regardless of how many precautionary layers of cashmere you may have adopted, and which mercifully obscures the view.

Twenty miles inland the sun may beat down warmly on some of the most magnificent country to be found within the British Isles, but in Carnoustie, when the haar rolls in from the North Sea, you know exactly how a bottle of champagne feels as it is plunged into an ice bucket. Haaaaar! How, you may ask, can life be supported in such a place? For many of us that is a fairly moot proposition, but the inhabitants have evolved a unique survival technique. It is based on the finest flowering of the Scottish culinary arts, an object resembling nothing so much in texture and taste and appearance (except for being yellow) as an ice-hockey puck. This is the infamous mutton pie. Human digestive juices can make no impression on it and, left to itself, it would simply remain in the system like an outsize gallstone.

However, generous measures of whisky will break down the mutton pie provided the mixture is well agitated. Hence, the inhabitants of Carnoustie make a daily pilgrimage to the foreshore and play golf, regardless of the weather. Now, a wonderful chemical process takes place. On reaction with the whisky, the mutton pie dissolves and spreads to the epidermis, forming an insulating layer akin to thermoplastic. The people of Carnoustie are thus double-glazed, as it were; or vulcanized, if you prefer. They go about their business with the minimum of clothing, remarking cheerfully to each other on what a bonny day it is.

The men of Carnoustie are fortified against all natural hardships and it was this quality which gave Carnoustie its special place in the history of golf, notably American golf. For towards the end of the last century, when golf in the United States was gathering momentum as a social craze of epidemic proportions, there was a chronic shortage of teachers and clubmakers to service the game.

Scotland, home of golf and economically depressed at the time, was the obvious source of golfing missionaries. The Atlantic steam packets were laden to the plimsoll line with migrant professionals. The village of Carnoustie (for such it was) sent some 150 of its sons to spread the gospel of golf in the New World.

How could a village produce so many pros? Well, in truth they were probably not all professional golfers in the sense we have come to understand the term. But for a Carnoustie boy, playing golf was as natural as breathing. It was something everyone did in the normal course of life.

The most famous of the Carnoustie immigrants were the

Smith brothers, Alex and Willie, who both won US Open Championships in due course, and Macdonald, reputedly a better but unluckier player than the lot of them.

One Carnoustie man did not make it. Legend has it that he decided to emigrate to South America, although in all probability that meant the southern states of America rather than the subcontinent. His friends gave him a lavish send-off party and, at a late hour, having downed a generous measure of mutton-pie-dissolving-fluid and with many a slurred promise to send the lads a card when he arrived, he staggered off into the night in the general direction of Dundee. The next thing he knew he was awaking, in an alcoholic haze, looking about him and remarking, 'So this is South America, I'd better build myself somewhere to live.' We do not know how far he progressed with his house-building before he realized his mistake, but one thing is certain. Far from being in South America, he was, in fact, only a mile away from Carnoustie, on the site of what is now the tenth hole, which is known as 'South America' to this day.

At a rather later date, another Carnoustie man successfully made the trip to America and caused a bigger stir than even the Smith brothers. That was Tommy Armour, who was blinded in one eye during World War I and who once climbed out of his tank to strangle a German with his bare hands. He brought some of that same directness of approach to his teaching of golf after his playing triumphs were over. Actually, it is cheating to call Armour a Carnoustie man, for he was born in Edinburgh, but when he returned to Scotland to win the Open at Carnoustie in 1931 it was too tempting a local-boy-makes-good story to quibble about a few miles.

At least, Armour brings us to the Open and to the links of Carnoustie. It is impossible to trace the origins of these old Scottish courses because in the beginning, in the fifteenth and sixteenth centuries, there was no formality about the layout of courses. You simply tucked your clubs (all wooden, of course) under your arm, put some balls in your pocket (featheries for the rich, boxwood for the poor) and went off to play over any promising golfing ground.

The land at Carnoustie was wild and bleak, and it still retains enough of an unkempt quality to justify Gary Player's horrified description of the course as 'a good swamp, spoiled'.

He should have seen it in 1527, when we have the first written record of golf at Carnoustie. A certain Sir Robert Maule was described as a devotee of hunting and hawking and 'he exersisit the gowf, and oft times to Barry Lynks quhan the wadsie was for drink'. For anyone not too well up in medieval Scottish, that means that he frequently played golf for a whisky-sour Nassau.

Even so, the finish was thought to be weak. In preparation for its inaugural Open, Carnoustie remodelled the closing holes to make a run-in of unrivalled severity.

Many clubs boast tough finishes. Merion, Pebble Beach and St Andrews are often cited as rugged examples. They are tame compared to Carnoustie, and especially in a teasing wind. Let us mentally play them together. The sixteenth is a par-3, satirically speaking, at 243 yards, as often as not needing a button-popping smash with a driver to a hog's-back green. The Barry Burn, which winds as insidiously as a tapeworm across the links, waits to swallow a hook or pull. On the right, a tangle of heather threatens a fate scarcely less painful. The sensible way to play this hole is to lay up with a 3-iron or so and hope to get down in a chip and a putt. But what golfer was ever that sensible?

Seventeen is worse. They call it the Island hole, a typical case of pawky Scottish wit because that Barry Burn snakes across the fairway four times, producing five possible islands on which you may choose to land your drive. On the tee you work out a complicated equation, involving your bicep size, courage rating and wind strength, and come up with a suggested target area. It was here that Jack Nicklaus once came tragically to grief. In the 1968 Open he had been playing his usual calculating, cautious game and he went into the fourth round trailing Gary Player. On the long sixth, Nicklaus hooked out of bounds, turned and kicked the bag out of his caddie's hands. Old Nicklaus watchers thrilled to the sight of this outburst. Now, Jack would forget all about safety and turn it on. He had to. And so he did, producing an exhibition of matchless shot-making. By the seventeenth he had Player in his sights and groggy. On the tee Nicklaus wound himself up and slugged the ball as hard as he could. The ball, flying all the convolutions of the burn, carried enough of the hole's 485 yards to leave him no more than a wedge to the flag. Player, laying up, had a 4-iron second shot.

It would be possible to draw up a list of fifty golfers almost guaranteed to birdie the hole after such a drive, but Nicklaus, with that toy wedge of his, would not get many votes as a pitcher of the ball, even from his own family. He duly made a hash of the shot, barely bobbling the ball to the front edge of the green. That gave Player the safety margin he needed.

Memory plays one false – and, anyway, you can look it up in the reference books if you are really interested – but the impression is that Player played the eighteenth in a series of nervous hops with his 7-iron. It was a par-5 then, with out of bounds all the way down the left, the infamous burn inter-secting the fairway three times, with the final twist just in front of the green to make you sweat, and rough up to your knees just for good measure.

That, then, is just one glimpse of Carnoustie. There are really 365 Carnousties, different golf courses with the varying weather each day of the year. Yesterday's clubbing is mean-ingless as a guide for today. Physically, it is the longest championship course in Britain at well over 7000 yards, but it can play as the shortest. The 1975 Open will be the fifth to be played over this capricious, unpredictable links. After Armour in 1931, Henry Cotton took the 1937 championship with a last-day 71 in a downpour. He played the finest golf of his life for that round of one under par. Then, in 1953, Ben Hogan entered for his one and only British Open. He won with descending rounds of 73, 71, 70, 68 in what many people hold to be the finest four rounds of competitive golf ever played in Britain. Lastly, as we have seen, Player took the title in 1968 after that heroic duel with Nicklaus.

Perhaps that roll of honour tells more about Carnoustie than any hole-by-hole description of the course. No one can anticipate what the 1975 Open will bring. Only one prediction is safe – that the winner will be a great player. It is certainly no place for mugs.

Carnoustie's last Open was the one previewed here, in 1975, which proved to be the first of Tom Watson's five victories in the Championship and the first of his eight majors. He won after a playoff with Jack Newton. Next year, 1999, the Open goes back to Carnoustie.

(GOLF WORLD 1975)

b.

The finest course of all

The late Bernard Darwin, the father of golf journalism, and, indeed, the pioneer along with Neville Cardus of literacy on the sports pages, was a considerable player as well as a fine essayist. When he sailed to America to cover the inaugural Walker Cup match, the captain fell ill and the man from *The Times* was co-opted to play and take over the duties of leading the side.

It was from Darwin that British golfers first learnt about Pine Valley. The course already had a fearsome local reputation by the time Darwin was taken there on a private visit in the twenties.

He played the first seven holes in level fours and then came comprehensively to grief at the eighth. He picked up his ball and, sad to relate, retired to the clubhouse after delivering judgment: 'It is all very well to punish a bad stroke, but the right of eternal punishment should be reserved for a higher tribunal than a green committee.'

So far as the outside world was concerned, that peppery diatribe set the tone for all subsequent writing about Pine Valley. The course had its label and there was no shortage of lurid anecdote to fuel that myth.

The members relished these horror stories and took pride in Pine Valley's growing notoriety as the most penal, the most difficult and the most malicious course in the world. They offered bets that visitors could not break 100 at the first attempt, or beat the par 18-up with the benefit of five strokes a hole.

So, my brain was thoroughly washed by doom and despondency before I set out for the backwoods of New Jersey to tilt my feeble lance at the gorgon of golf. A friend sped me on the way with the words: 'It is all very well for golfers of Walker Cup calibre, but for the likes of you and I it is simply unplayable.'

As to that, and to all the rest of the weeping and wailing and spitting of blood about Pine Valley, I am now ready to respond with a cheery cry of 'Rubbish!' True, it demands a standard of accuracy which is beyond most golfers, myself near the top of the list. Equally true, it exacts a scale of punishment which is positively Old Testament in its severity, six strokes being a common sanction for missing a fairway or one of the greens which rise like islands in a sea of unraked sand.

As for the bunkers, there is one turf-walled brute at the front of the short tenth whose name is prudishly rendered in official publications as the Devil's Advocate or the Devil's Pit or, getting closer to the truth of the matter, the Devil's, ah, Aperture, or just DAH. It is about eight feet in diameter and the same depth, with steps set into the sand to assist the exhausted and disgruntled golfer to get back to the surface at the end of his shift.

One player, accomplished enough to have scored 35 on the first nine holes, found this bunker off the tee and took 23 for the hole. Devilish intervention caused one four-ball to run up an aggregate of 88 strokes at the tenth and another player, having ruined his card and his disposition by taking seven strokes to extricate his ball from the pit, sat on its rim with his feet dangling into the abyss and howled like a baby.

My favourite Pine Valley story is of the four-ball which lost one of its members in the woods. Three of them sliced into the trees and the fourth hooked his ball wildly. After playing back into the open country, the three slicers crossed the fairway to help their companion's search. They found his ball but he was nowhere to be seen.

The police delivered him back to the clubhouse late at night, somewhat the worse for drink. He had lost his bearings and wandered for miles through the forest, and had celebrated his eventual contact with civilisation in the time honoured tradition of *après* golf.

All these tales – and everyone who has enjoyed the privilege of playing Pine Valley has a personal disaster to relate – bear out the horrific reputation of the course. But they tell only the lesser half of the story. Because of the perils which beset the golfer on every side, the charge of exhilaration he receives when he successfully carries his drive over 170 yards of sandy waste is proportionately increased.

The hitting of a green, a routine enough experience at your home club, becomes a thrill. As for holing across those undulating greens with surfaces as slick as polished marble, watching the ball swing as much as twenty feet on its roller coaster route, the afterglow of achievement lasts for weeks.

So, while playing Pine Valley can be a penance, and nearly always is somewhere during the round, the agonies are the price which must be paid for the ecstasies. Provided you leave your ego back in the locker room, Pine Valley is a delight. The scenery alone is intoxicating and enhanced by the wildlife of what is in effect a 650-acre nature reserve.

When my friend asks what I scored, he will doubtless say, 'I told you that you could never get around it.' In terms of numbers, that is a just comment, but numbers, far from being the be all and end all of golf, are the least part of the game.

After Pine Valley, by a long way the finest course I have experienced, other courses will seem humdrum, so I may very likely retire, to take up pursuits more suited to my creaking bones. It would be a pity to end on a high score but fitting to go out on the highest note of them all.

Of all the professional accolades bestowed on Peter during his life, none meant more to him than being made an honorary overseas member of Pine Valley. It was in 1985 that the club opened its fabled course to its most public scrutiny ever, by staging the Walker Cup.

(OBSERVER 1985)

Mini golf can be a major thrill

Municipal and pay-and-play courses claim to offer cheap golf for the masses. In fact, in many instances the cost of playing regularly on a public course works out as high or higher than the membership fees for a private club.

But what if there was some way of getting into golf without having to lay out two month's wages to equip yourself for the game? And then, what if you could play a round for the price of a burger and a pint of beer?

Does that sound like pie in the sky? Not a bit of it. They have had it like that in Ireland for sixty years. Pitch-and-Putt is an offshoot of golf, a separate game in its own right with an independent governing body.

Instead of requiring 150 acres, a Pitch-and-Putt course of eighteen holes fits easily into four acres. The course cannot exceed 900 metres and the maximum length for a hole is 70 metres. Players may carry only two clubs, one of which must be a putter.

Because you do not spend so much time walking, the game is more concentrated than golf and eighteen holes can be completed well inside an hour. The game has two other major advantages over golf; men and women can compete on equal terms and it can be played from a wheelchair.

There is a common perception that Pitch-and-Putt is the poor relation of golf, a miniaturized and inferior version of the real thing. And it has to be admitted that many of Ireland's four hundred Pitch-and-Putt courses, many attached to pubs, are so basic, just rudimentary greens dotted around an open field, as to be unappealing.

Trees and shrubs add enormously to the appearance and strategic challenge of Pitch-and-Putt courses, and I am glad to see that in Australia, where the game is growing fast under the energetic direction of Sean Lynch, great attention is being paid to making new courses look attractive.

These days, when waking up in the morning involves completing a ritual check list to discover which parts of the body are functioning properly, the notion of Pitch-and-Putt golf becomes increasingly appealing.

We are all popularly supposed to remember what we were doing on the day of President Kennedy's assassination. My memories are especially vivid because I was a minor functionary, albeit I believed myself to be a big-shot editor at the time, on a mass-circulation newspaper in London. We had five pages of biography on the presses within twenty minutes, and that was just the start of the most intensive, hectic and stimulating eight hours of work of my life.

Eventually, I got to my bed just as the birds were starting to bellow their dawn chorus. The following conversation then ensued:

WIFE: 'I bought a house today.'

SELF: 'Uhu.'

WIFE: 'I think you'll like it.'

SELF: 'Zzzzzzz.'

As it happened, I did like the place. In fact, I liked it so much that I bought an extra piece of land at the end of the garden for no better reason than that the price was right. One day we would think of something to do with it.

That day arrived a month or so ago, by which time the land was so thickly overgrown with trees and scrub that only the resident foxes and badgers could penetrate it.

It is not big enough for a conventional Pitch-and-Putt course, but since there will never be more than one match on it at a time, I can have the fairways crossing each other as much as I need to accommodate nine holes covering 450 metres.

My life is now dedicated to creating the most beautiful Pitch-and-Putt course in the world. The site is land-locked, making it impossible to get any form of mechanical appliance onto the ground. The mammoth task of slashing and burning and digging up tree stumps and tilling and sowing will all have to be done by hand.

So be it. The work will take longer but the end result will be all the more satisfying for having been irrigated by the sweat of my brow. I like to think that my private folly might give others the idea of creating public Pitch-and-Putt courses which would bring the pleasures of golf to a whole new community who otherwise could never afford to try their hands at this absorbing pastime.

Meanwhile, I have enough grandchildren to indoctrinate in the ways of golf and provide me with opponents. That prospect is justification enough for building my course. It also provides a twist on an old saying, enabling me to boast: 'There is a fairyland at the bottom of my garden.'

This was written at the end of 1993; the consequent Pitch-and-Putt course Peter built – Royal Pratts Bottom, as it semi-inevitably became called, in recognition of the extraordinarily named village in Kent where Peter lived – became his pride and joy. In May 1996, he hosted a competition for his friends there (the nine-hole event was won by Jerry Tarde, editor of Golf Digest *in the United States). Peter, although clearly not strong, talked then of going to Oakmont for the US Open the next month. Not many of us thought he would make it, but he did. It was the last major championship he attended.*

(GOLF WORLD 1994)

The European experience

Golf on the continent is nearly always a rewarding experience and some of my happiest memories involve the unique local flavour of the game across the Channel and the North Sea. However, time spent on reconnaissance is never wasted and, if a personal reminiscence may be permitted, I shall begin with a cautionary tale. It might be said without excessive disloyalty that my wife falls into the category of women which the late Henry Longhurst described as playing golf to give them something to think about while they are talking. She and a friend make regular forays to one of the local munis and as often as not return cursing the lack of consideration of men or seeking a ruling about whether a stroke must be counted when throwing a ball back to the fairway from behind an equally inconsiderate tree.

They more than make up for any slight deficiencies in technique with their enthusiasm and, since I am in a constant state of shuttling from tournament to tournament during the summer, they decided to have a week's golfing holiday in Spain. The glossy brochure – ah, those brochures! – painted an idyllic picture: 'free' transport to the course, 'free' golf and unlimited sunshine.

There was no transport, and when they made their way to the course they were peremptorily informed that they must wait until two more players arrived since it was compulsory to play in fours. As luck would have it, the next arrivals happened to be two young stockbrokers, both scratch. It is a moot point which of the two parties was the more aghast at the prospect of the next six hours and only impeccable Home Counties breeding saved the day. 'Three for you, Jeremy, and what about you, partner? Let's see. Four up to the trap, nine out, two in the water, chip, putt, three in the sand and two putts.'

The moral is to check the small print or, even better, to go native and throw yourself into the swim of the local golf. The one common denominator throughout the wide world of golf is a kindly disposition to see that a visitor gets fixed up with a game.

If some fortunate golfer announced that he proposed an extended tour of Europe and sought my advice as to an itinerary, money no object, I would counsel starting in Sweden, or anywhere in Scandinavia, in order to minimize the culture shock. The courses are mainly cut through pine forests although, appearances apart, the tone and style of Swedish golf very much resembles the Scottish tradition, except that the Swedes speak better English. Because they are denied golf and all other outdoor sports for six months of the year, the Swedes get stir-crazy and, when the days do begin to lengthen, they hate to waste one minute of precious daylight. They believe in cheap golf and concentrate their resources on the courses rather than pretentious clubhouses and frills. They go off at dawn and snatch a hurried sandwich before going out again, revelling in hitting the ball vast distances.

The Swedes are impatient for national success at golf, to follow their impact on tennis, and are tremendously supportive of junior golf, which makes a refreshing change from the grudging attitude to juniors which we adopt in Britain. So, golf in Sweden is exhilarating, exhausting and you can forget all ideas about boisterous dinners in the club afterwards. The nation is positively neurotic about drinking and driving and the price of booze is prohibitive. Bear up, you will have worked up a formidable thirst for your next sample of European golf.

They know how to drink in Germany, especially in Bavaria, which also happens to be prime golfing country. In spite of

Bernhard Langer's international acclaim, golf in Germany remains a minority sport and there is only one public course the country. The ecologists, who are extremely influential, deter the local authorities from creating municipal golf, which is doubly sad because a well-designed course is one of the best nature reserves that can be created, as well as an arboretum, and, surprising as this may seem, it provides more recreation per person, per hour, per acre than a tennis court or a soccer pitch. It can also act as an urban lung or a guarantee of conserving green-belt land, not to mention the source of valuable municipal income. If the ecologists really informed themselves on their subject, instead of responding with a knee-jerk cry of 'Touch not a single tree', they would be advocates of golf courses rather than opponents.

The Germans who do play are immensely dedicated, absolute sticklers for the rules and tireless in pursuit of correct technique. The teachers make fortunes. Many times I have been asked to arbitrate between conflicting theories. When Toski says this, John Jacobs says that and Henry Cotton says the other. Which is the correct way? The concept that there are many different truths in golf offends the logical German mind. There is therefore an air of formality on the course, but once the game is over the players unbend and the visitor needs a strong constitution to keep pace with the foaming steins of beer. I would suggest Munich as a good base, both for the golf and the riotous assembly afterwards.

There are two forms of golf in France and the visitor must make his choice according to taste. In the Basque country along the Spanish border around Biarritz, they have been playing golf since the Duke of Wellington arrived for a bit of R&R after the Peninsular War.

The Basques are a mysterious people. Nobody knows where they came from, nobody understands their language and nobody knows why they make such exceptional sportsmen. Their own game, *pelote Basque*, is the supreme sporting expression of athleticism, instant responses and dextrous skills but they seem to take to all sports. All the best French golfers and rugby players are Basques, and the golf clubs are pretty much in the British tradition of putting the game first, with the trimmings very much in the practical rather than ornate style. So, the British visitor will feel at home, unless he is fortunate enough to acquire the services of a fisherman's wife as a caddie. These splendid creatures, swathed all in black, make perfect caddies in that they have eyes like hawks to follow the errant ball and never speak. They like to get on with the game, which suits my natural tempo on the course, in order to get home and prepare the *bouillabaise* for the old man's supper.

In the rest of France, particularly around Paris where the game is concentrated, they play designer golf, just as they drink designer water and wear designer clothes. Elegance is everything and the visitor gets the feeling that the score is less important than successfully matching your cardigan to your angora head covers. The clubhouse is likely to be a chateau and, while some of the courses are excellent, you have the impression that the really significant element is the Harry Colt label. I always feel like a peasant in those tastefully opulent surroundings and am happy to settle for such a designation. After all, I know all too well that if I did dress up and rolled into the car park in a hired Mercedes, I would be instantly categorized as a *nouveau riche* peasant, so why bother?

Swiss golf is mainly centred around Geneva. It is swish, expensive and rather Parisian. However, there is one bargain in summer and that is high in the Alps at Crans-sur-Sierre, where they play the European Masters. This is basically a ski resort for the beautiful people, with Bond Street price tags and luxury hotels. The golf course was created to maintain a flow of tourists after the snows had melted and it presents a gorgeous panorama of white-topped Alps, with the Rhone glinting far below like a silver snake in the hazy valley. For those who give a high priority to the surroundings as a component of golf pleasure, Crans is a collector's item and the off-season prices are reasonable. You will probably have to make up a match with other visitors because the Swiss do not waste a lot of time on frivolous pursuits, their purpose in life being to man the till.

Spain used to be the golfer's paradise but the Costa del Sol became so popular that it all went wrong, temporarily I trust. Demand exceeded supply and, while the courses are excellent, too many people had experiences such as the one I outlined at the beginning. It is almost entirely tourist golf, so the chances of playing with Spanish golfers are remote.

My personal recommendation would be to make a base in one of the superb tourist hotels run by the government, usually converted castles, and to play day after day on one of the world's finest masterpieces, El Saler, on the coast near Valencia. It is operated by the local authority, which makes it reasonable, and offers one of the great golfing experiences of Europe.

Holidaymakers who have become disillusioned by six-hour rounds and rip-off green fees on the Costa del Sol have transferred their allegiance to Portugal and the Algarve coast. The undiscovered delights of the Algarve are now under threat of over-popularity and costs are rising.

Portugal is the pro-am capital of Europe and, while such events are harmless diversions in theory, they do tend to degenerate at times into sporting versions of the more acrimonious debates at the United Nations. The blood pressure on these occasions rises in direct ratio to the value of the prizes and the dishonesty of the handicaps. Pro-am promoters work on the basis that the only way they can charge the punters through the nose is to put up prizes which would give the chairman of the Amateur Status Committee a fit of hysterics. The lure of this booty in turn creates a brisk market in forged handicap certificates.

The British are eccentric enough over handicaps, the English snobbishly denying themselves their due allotment of strokes, so that they boast modestly, 'I am supposed to be single figures at George's, for my sins. Absolutely ridiculous, but there it is,' while the Scots and Irish pad their handicaps a stroke or two in order to win money off the hated English. Fair enough. These conceits and deceits are relatively petty.

But the continentals! They bring to the subject of handicaps the same soaring imagination and chicanery as they apply to the completion of their income tax returns. At times the scale of deception can be breathtaking in its enormity. I well remember the innocent young son of an international *bandito* telling me that his millionaire father refused to join a club, preferring to pay green fees in order to avoid being allocated an official certificate which would be at variance with his self-imposed handicap of 24. My estimate was that he played to about eight.

Even more brazen was the two-handicap woman who entered a big pro-am off a handicap of 22, the margin of her victory being so absurd that her duplicity was instantly exposed. It does not take many such individual incidents for the reputation of an entire nation to become besmirched, which is why the conversation at prize-giving parties tends to be *sotto voce* and violently xenophobic. The ideal of international good-will through sport takes a terrible hammering. Say the French: 'The group in front were German so we had to wait on every shot, naturally'. Say the Germans: 'Those French! What else can you expect?' Say the Swiss: 'Are those the winners? Italians, no doubt.' Say the Dutch: 'Did you see what those Swedes were wearing? Disgusting!' The British escape relatively unscathed from the verbal assassinations, not because of any national popularity but because they seldom get among the silverware.

Of course, the contestants at major international pro-ams are by definitions well off and the state of being rich does seem to go with being more or less unspeakable, regardless of nationality. Real golfers, in my experience, are much the same the world over. Martyrdom to a chronic slice transcends boundaries and infirmities with the short putts forming a universal bond.

You may wonder why I have crisscrossed Europe without once mentioning Holland, where the game began. The reason for this neglect does not mean that I have anything against the Dutch. It is just that as a golfer I do not consider Holland to be foreign. Imagine, if you can, that the Royal and Ancient Golf Club of St Andrews decided to expand and create a chain of golf clubs. Just as your High Street version of Harrods would recreate the atmosphere of the Knightsbridge original in like eventuality, so Dutch golf clubs resemble nothing so much as outposts of the R&A.

The courses are uniformly good, the quarters comfortable and modest and the conversation tends to discussions on recondite points of golf politics. I happen to have a special admiration for Van Dyke but have never had much success with him as a topic in a Dutch golf club. 'Wasn't that the chap who made such a hash of the short hole in the home internationals at Georges?' I mean, why go abroad if you find yourself back home when you get there? Travel can only broaden the mind if it exposes the traveller to fresh and exotic experiences, which brings me to my favourite European golfing country.

Italy tends to broaden the figure as much as the mind but it is gloriously foreign. Golf is not so much a game as an aid to digestion. My introduction to the Italian way of golf was at Garlenda, in the foothills of the Italian Riviera, whence I travelled for the nominal purpose of reporting a tournament for my newspaper.

This task involves following the play, talking to the players and then writing a coherent account of the day's events. That is the theory, anyway. On this occasion, arriving at about noon, I was offered an aperitif and then invited to partake of lunch. Why not, I thought. A quick bite and I would be clear in time to go out with the leaders. The room to which I was directed was furnished with a table running its entire length and bearing a massive proliferation of delicious dishes. Golly, I thought, this is what I call a buffet, as I heaped my plate. No sooner had the last anchovy slithered to the destination designated for it by nature's grand design than a white-coated figure took my plate and bade me follow him. He led me to the adjacent dining room where each place setting, as well as the usual cutlery, included a bottle of Chianti and a bottle of Barolo, both of which the waiter proceeded to open.

The waiter offered me a choice of five varieties of pasta. Although replete, I remembered the blurb about when in Rome and forced myself to accommodate a large plate of *spaghetti alla carbonara*. Takes a bit of washing down, that stuff. The waiter solicited my desire for a main course. On his advice, I went for the porco. '*Dolce*? The *zabaglione* is excellent.' So it was. By now all vestiges of self-control had vanished and the ordeal had taken the form of a challenge, and I had the national reputation to uphold. When you think of the labour and time that goes into the creation of a fine vintage – all that pruning and trampling the grapes – it seems a shame to spurn it. Besides, it helped the cheese go down. The sight of the coffee was as welcome as a lifeboat to a drowning man but that was not quite the end of it. The large *strega* seem to be obligatory.

I reeled out to the golf course, gastric gases exploding from every orifice, to walk off that gargantuan feast. It occurred to me that this must have been a special occasion, laid on by the sponsor to suborn the professional integrity of the press. During subsequent visits to Italy I discovered that this was a rather modest lunch by the standards of golf clubs. Eating and drinking is the purpose of the golf club, the course is just where you go to walk off your three-hour binge. 'How was the golf, dear?' 'Not bad. A shade too much oregano in the veal sauce on the front nine but I sank some terrific asparagus tips towards the end.'

The only complication for the visitor, and it is not a serious one, is that you cannot set foot on an Italian course unless you have a title. They are cheap enough to buy, in the pro's shop I shouldn't wonder ('Three Titleists and a barony, *per favore*'), but there is an easier way. If you have an item of luggage made of real leather and hand stitched, or an article of clothing from Savile Row – they have an eye for such things – the staff will automatically call you *dottore* and that will do. They will also assume you to be impoverished, since such is the natural state of the aristocracy in Italy, and will be pathetically grateful for the stingiest of tips. For them it is an honour to serve such a fine gentleman. Can you wonder why Italy is my favourite stomping ground for golf? As for playing with the Italians, they have a splendidly aristocratic disregard of those bourgeois rules and tend to shout a lot. 'Is your ball playable, count?' 'Not yet.'

If anyone should be hesistating about whether to go golfing on the continent, wondering whether he might fit in with those foreigners, my advice is to take the plunge. You may not fit in, but if you are prepared to leave your prejudices in the locker room and go along with the local way of golf, then you will have a terrific time. In the kingdom of golf there are many mansions and they are all rewarding in their different ways. My apologies to Norway, Finland, Austria, Denmark, Greece, Belgium, etc., but lack of space precludes further insults. They all offer golf of distinctive national flavours, but you will just have to go and sample them for yourselves.

Give Peter a wide brief – like 'How about a piece on golf in Europe?' – and the result would often be hilarious.

(GOLF WORLD 1986)

FOUR: COMMERCIAL BREAK

The 'Olde English Breakfast'
conquers the world.

In the beginning

A script for 'That Was The Week, That Was' – TW3 – written with Peter Lewis to mark the opening of the London Hilton hotel.

In the beginning there was darkness upon the face of the earth and there was no iced water. And Hilton said, 'Let there be iced water,' and in every bathroom, pipes ran with plenteous iced water and Hilton saw that it was good. Then he said, 'Let there be music,' and in every lobby, single studio parlour, double French bedroom and luxury suite, nay, in every elevator, other pipes gushed with plenteous canned music. And Hilton said, 'Let the earth bring forth Hiltons, yielding fruit after their kind.' And the El Paso Hilton begat the Beverly Hilton, which begat the Puerto Rico Hilton which begat the Istanbul Hilton which begat the Panama Hilton which begat the Berlin Hilton which begat the Nile Hilton which begat the Virgin Isles Hilton which begat the Trinidad Hilton which begat the Teheran Hilton which begat the Acapulco Hilton and on the seventh day Hilton rested . . . but only for a moment.

For messengers came unto him and said, 'Behold, there is an Anglo-Saxon people that dwell in darkness and know not thy name, nor drink they of thine iced water.' And Hilton took out his rod and smote upon the rock in the place they call Park Lane and out of it came forth a pillar of 130,000 cubic feet of concrete. And the view from the top thereof was thirty miles in any direction and from thirty miles in any direction thereof the view was, alas, of the pillar.

Then sent Hilton for the scribes and elders of the people and commanded them to come to him. And they cast lots and sent unto him an elder named Maudling whom they could best spare to be sacrificed. And he gave him a pair of silver scissors and bade him cut the tape, and Maudling would not. But the serpent Clore, who privily did own the freehold, tempted his handmaiden, Beryl, and she spake unto Maudling saying: 'Give me the scissors.' And lo, as he stood pondering as was his wont, what words to speak, she cut the tape and there was a great gushing of iced water and puking of piped music and a great charging of fifty guineas a night without breakfast.

And Hilton said, 'Behold, I have given you the London Hilton containing everything meet for your needs: a view into the garden of your Queen, yea, and a library wherein ye may read Hilton Milton and 850 Hilton menservants and maidservants smiling Hilton smiles, which they smile not saying cheese, as other men, but saying Hilton Stilton.'

But the people were a stiff-necked people who would not drink of the iced water nor would they eat of the Olde English Breakfast, consisting of ripe melon, All Bran, crisp waffles with ham or sausage and hot chocolate. For they cried out, 'What is this Olde English Breakfast, for we know it not, neither will we pay 15s 6d for it.'

And Hilton was exceeding wrath and departed with a gnashing of teeth to beget the Athens Hilton which begat the Moscow Hilton which was called the Comrade Hilton which begat the Pisa Hilton which was called the Tiltin' Hilton which begat the Tel Aviv Hilton which was called the Hilton Schmilton which begat the Rabat Hilton and doubtless also the Sodom Hilton and Gomorrah Hilton which were also turned into pillars of concrete. And it came to pass that the Hiltons covered the face of the earth and there was a great flood of iced water and the darkness was greater than it was in the beginning.

Not without honour

A TW3 script which suggests that, while these days it may be Tony Blair rather than Harold Wilson in Downing Street, the mechanics of government have not changed altogether.

MAN ENTERS STAGE LEFT WITH LETTER AND READS:

Sir, I am asked by the Prime Minister to inform you that he has it in mind on the occasion of the forthcoming list of birthday honours to submit your name to the Queen with a recommendation that she may be graciously pleased to approve that you be appointed a Knight Commander of the Order of the British Empire ...

BLACKOUT. SIMULTANEOUSLY THE LIGHTS GO UP ON TWO MEN ENTERING STAGE RIGHT CARRYING GOLF BAGS. AS THEY TALK THEY APPROACH AN IMAGINARY GOLF TEE CENTRE STAGE, UNHITCH THEIR CLUBS, TEE-UP, ADDRESS THE BALL AND DRIVE OFF IN TURN. AFTER DRIVING AND WATCHING THE FLIGHT OF THE IMAGINARY BALLS, THEY PICK UP THEIR CLUBS AND WALK OFF TOGETHER, WALKING ON THE SPOT UNTIL THEY STOP FOR THE SECOND STROKE. AND SO FORTH. NO REFERENCE IS MADE TO THE GAME AT ALL.

X: You know, old Coggers is expecting his peerage this year.
Y: Coggers. Good heavens, I'd clean forgotten about him.
X: Well, you remember what we told him the last time we were getting the list ready for the PM. We can't keep on leaving him out.
Y: But look here, wasn't he in charge of that West African sisal scheme? How much did it lose? £35 million or something.

X: Oh come now, be reasonable. If we went on the basis of no profit no honour, Debrett would soon be coming out as a paperback.

Y: And you and I would be out of a job.

X: Exactly.

Y: I suppose you'd better put him down. How many does that leave us?

X: Well, clearing out the deadwood in the Cabinet is going to clear up most of the baronies, Harold's got a couple of viscountcies up his sleeve, left owing from last year's shooting parties.

Y: Then there's the constituency position to think of. There's Waterton. We need his seat for young Satterthwaite, so he'll have to go upstairs for one.

X: Seems a shame really. Waterton's worked hard, and I never could see any sign of ability in young Satterthwaite.

Y: No point in arguing. Lady B plays duets with him. She wants him in and that's that.

X: Then there's Cubby Broccoli.

Y: Lord yes, put him down. He'll never hold East Bristol. Fought four elections with ever-decreasing majorities. Scraped in by 110 last time. It's obviously time we relieved him of the necessity of winning votes. Well, that pretty well takes care of the Upper House.

X: Except for Higginbotham.

Y: What on earth do you mean, Higginbotham?

X: Higginbotham definitely expects something. Hints have been dropped.

Y: My dear fellow, we can't start putting in people like Higginbotham. I remember him as a fag. Nasty, snotty-nosed little bounder. Never changed his vest. Stole my rugger boots once. Put him in the Lords? Not on your life.

X: Well, he does own most of Birmingham, Walsall and Lombard Street. All those ghastly office blocks going up are his, you know.

Y: But you can't just *buy* your way in, by God. I just won't hear of Higginbotham and there's an end of it.

X: All right, all right. But I think you may change your mind. Now, what about the knights? McNorton's been mentioned to me. Thirty years in public life and never given the least offence to anybody.

Y: Yes, very civil fellow. I think we might make that a baronetcy, don't you? He's been very docile.

X: Then there's Prosser. Chairman of that infernal committee always poking its nose in where it isn't wanted and making damn fool recommendations. I had a word with the PMG at the club the other day and he made it pretty clear we could remove a nasty thorn in his side by elevating Prosser.

Y: Odious fellow. A knighthood's too good. Give him an OBE to show him what we think of him. What about the beatniks? We've got the usual list of bearded wonders from the Arts Council and Lady B's found some new composers. Oh, CBEs, CBEs, I always class them with local aldermen, county surveyors and association footballers. After all, stringing notes together's not on the same plane as cricket. How are we doing for dames, by the way?

X: Oh, Perkins is scouting round Oxford and Cambridge for a few dames. I've left him to look after all the small stuff, too. MBEs and so on.

Y: I suppose we've lined up plenty of chars and long-serving railwaymen?

X: Yes. Though chars are getting a bit difficult. There was one last year at the Treasury who kept leaving hers on the Chancellor's desk with a note saying she'd rather have wages in lieu.

Y: Still, as a whole, they're a pretty dull lot. We'd better put in one or two for the newspapers. Who have we got left in the theatre?

X: Been a bit reckless there lately, I'm afraid. Hardly any knightable actors left. We could start on the playwrights, I suppose.

Y: I say, here's an idea for livening things up. Give a peerage to Michael Foot.

X: Mm ... not a cat in hell's chance of working that one. These Labour boys are very wary these days. Remember old Wedgy Benn.

Y: Ah, but we can get round that. Make it life. And no remission for good conduct.

X: Well, I'll have a word with Hugh about it. I rather fancy we can count on his support for one. Now to come back to Higginbotham for a moment ...

Y: I've told you once, you *can't* make that shady operator a peer. Just think of it, *Lord* Higginbotham.

X: Oh, he can disguise it by choosing a suitable locality to be baron of. Somewhere like Burnham Beeches or Virginia Water or Boulter's Lock.

Y: Knowing Higginbotham it's more likely to be Wolverhampton or Chalk Farm or the Birkenhead Ferry. He'll want concrete mixers on his coat of arms and a motto like 'Semper in Excreto'.

X: Well, I think the PM is expecting his name to appear.

Y: Over my dead body. (HE PUTTS AND WATCHES THE BALL INTO THE HOLE.) In she goes. What a delightful course this is. My hole, I think.

X: Good shot. Yes, your hole. Until next week, that is. After that it'll be Higginbotham's hole.

Y: What on earth do you mean?

X: You weren't at the last club meeting, were you? Pity. Higginbotham's bought an option on all this land for a huge new dormitory suburb. Forty-storey blocks of flats. Shame the old course will have to go.

Y: He's got to be stopped. How's he going to be stopped?

X: Well, he hinted pretty broadly he could be put off only by the most powerful considerations. The sort of considerations we are in a position to supply.

Y: Well, don't just stand there. Go and get him on the telephone.

The resignation

*Another governmental script. Obviously fiction, though. Who-
ever resigns these days?*

My Dear Prime Minister,
  It is with deep regret that I have to tell you that I feel the time
has now come for me to lay down the burden of office. It has
been my honour and privilege to serve under your inspiring
leadership for more than fifty years, and I can say with pride
that I have never wavered in my support for you on both sides
of all the great issues of our times, in peace and in both wars,
that of 1914 no less than that of 1900. Through good times and
bad we have marched and slept side by side on the back
benches, on the front benches and across the cabinet table.
Seldom, I can truly say, has a team of ministers been, in quite so
literal sense, one big happy family. Nevertheless, we must
recognize that the time may well have come to make way for
an older man. May I assure you for the future that you may
always depend on my unthinking support.

My Dear Goofy,
  Thank you very much for your letter. You know how deeply
you regret my decision. You have been a most loyal colleague
and it is a great sorrow to me to feel that I shall no longer have
you to lean on in the course of our deliberations. Throughout
your long career of inconspicuous public service you have
never spared yourself, or the country, approaching all our
tasks with an open, indeed blank, mind. You will be long
remembered as a robust Minister of Health, an immovable
Minister of Transport and an inedible Minister of Food. You
showed that ignorance is no handicap at the Ministry of
Education and at the Ministry of Labour you demonstrated

that indolence is no crime. To the Ministry of Pensions you brought that invaluable qualification, age, and you have always worked untiringly for our relations with the Commonwealth by finding untiring work in the Commonwealth for our relations. Finally, as a whip, you cracked. I know I speak for the country when I say that your departure from the public scene will come as a well-earned relief.

This'll kill you

*The argument about banning cigarettes has in some respects
hardly advanced in getting on for forty years.*

For forty-three years now I've been selling carcinogens.
Not wittingly, mind you. Not wittingly for all that time.
When I first took this kiosk there wasn't any harm in tobacco.
People smoked ... and died ... and nobody kept on at them
about it. So I didn't worry unduly when the first scare started
just after the war. There's always somebody trying to spoil
other people's pleasures. Didn't somebody put the wind up the
Romans by telling them there was a limit to the number of
times men and women could ... well, there was a limit anyway
and if they went over the ration ... phffft! That belief proved
ill-founded, as many of you are no doubt aware.

I reckoned it would be the same story with fags. Then the
General Medical Council looked into it and said there wasn't
any doubt about it whatever. *And* the Government accepted
their report. Well ... I was worried for a time. Not for myself,
mind, I don't smoke, but I felt sorry for all those rats and mice.
Besides, this kiosk is my living. But as it turned out, I needn't
have worried at all. My takings actually went up that year.

One of my customers would have his little joke. 'Death
sentences,' he'd say. 'That's what you're selling. There ought to
be a law against people like you,' he said when he came to
collect his box of fifty every morning. Very comical character. I
was sorry to see him go. I said to Doris after the funeral, I said,
'Supposing they did pass a law? What ought we to do?'

'Don't you worry,' she said. 'Just you wait till the Government tells us what to do. Course they'll stop you selling fags if
they're harmful,' she said. 'But they'll give us compensation.
You can trust the Government.' That was her favourite phrase,

God rest her soul. She put her head in the gas oven when her bit of War Loan fell to 53.

Well, this other report came out so I took the problem to our MP. A more straightforward man you could not hope to meet. 'Don't you worry, Armitage,' he said. 'The Government won't ban the sale of tobacco for one very good reason,' he said. 'Because it would be interfering with the liberty of the subject. There's twenty million smokers in the country,' he said. 'Now would it be fair to *them*? There is also the consideration that the tobacco tax brings in £830 million a year, which is 14 per cent of the annual revenue and we just couldn't carry on without it.'

Well, when he put it like that, I could see it was my patriotic duty to keep the kiosk open. If we closed down, you wouldn't have no hydrogen bombs and that. If you look at it, as these MPs do, impartially, 27,000 deaths a year from lung cancer is a small price to pay for the liberty of the subject *plus* a nuclear stockpile.

Twenty thousand people represents the population of quite a small town, like Newbury, say. Ah! I can see what you're thinking: Newbury last year, Windsor this year, Abingdon, Wallingford, Lambourn, Streatley and Pangbourne next year ... a few more years and we'll have got through the whole of Berkshire. But it's no use running away from the facts. Berkshire, pleasant as it is, has to be weighed against the long-term welfare of the country as a whole.

So I don't worry, and if you take my tip, you won't worry either. If you feel like a carcinogen, you go right ahead and have one.

You've got the law on your side. You've got the Government behind you. And you're making your contribution to the defence of Britain and the cause of liberty, for which so many of your fellow-smokers have not hesitated to lay down their lives.

Doctor-speak

TW3 again on the health beat. Another script with Peter Lewis.

There is no profession like medicine for saying one thing and meaning another. For example:

DOCTOR SAYS: I think you'd better have a day or two in hospital so we can keep an eye on that foot.
THINKS: We'll have to amputate.
DOCTOR SAYS: Don't worry about that tickling sensation in your right foot, it'll disappear in a day or two.
THINKS: We have amputated your right foot.
DOCTOR SAYS: I don't know whether you read the small type at the bottom of that consent form you signed before the operation.
THINKS: We've amputated the wrong foot.
DOCTOR SAYS: Tell me if you feel a sharp pain when I press here. (PRESSING STOMACH)
THINKS: That missing scalpel must be *somewhere*.
DOCTOR SAYS: See how you get on with these pills and come back and see me in a couple of days.
THINKS: I'm due on the first tee in a couple of minutes.
DOCTOR SAYS: All right, you can put your clothes on now, Miss Loren.
THINKS: So who cares if the money isn't so good?
DOCTOR SAYS: (INTO PHONE) Do you realize it is two in the morning? Try an aspirin.
THINKS: I'm emigrating to Australia next week.
DOCTOR: SAYS: Never mind about it being two in the morning. I'll be straight round.
THINKS: I am a West Indian.

Unaccustomed as I am ...

From a speech delivered by Peter at Ferndown Golf Club, near Bournemouth, in 1993.

I have psychic powers. I can read minds. At this moment you are asking yourselves the question: 'Who is the old fart about to bore our tits off?'

I will give you a quick run down. I took up golf as a boy but my early progress was interrupted by the onset of puberty and World War II.

That was long before the permissive age, of course. In those days, no nice girl would dream of going the whole hog, as they called it in the convent. But I noticed there was one exception to this strict moral code. If a young man came along with a pair of wings on his tunic, the nicest of girls positively hurled herself at him with legs akimbo.

I immediately volunteered for flying training. You will want to know whether I had a 'good' war. Well, in the sense that I won ...

When it was all over, I had the usual interview with the careers officer. He looked at my records and said, 'You've got no education, no qualifications and no scruples. You'd best stand for Parliament.' He could see I wasn't too keen on politics by the way I threw up. 'In that case,' he said, 'there's nothing else for it but the press.'

I became a golf columnist. You probably know the duties of a columnist. He hides in the mountains during the height of the battle and then comes down and bayonets the wounded.

Everyone has a clear idea of what the life of a golf writer is like. You shoot off to exotic places in the sun at somebody else's expense. You play golf every morning. Then, you go to the course and get a few quotes from the leader. You send a garbled version over to your newspaper and now you are ready for the most torrid evening of wild debauchery that the local town can offer. Boy, did we ever look forward to covering tournaments at Ferndown.

With a routine like that you get to hone your game to a peak of perfection. So, you may be surprised to learn that in all my thirty-odd years of competitive golf, I only ever won one major championship. That was a long time ago but you can still read the faded inscription on the trophy: 'Wash your balls with a Spontex sponge'.

There are two hazards involved in being a golf writer. Fifty per cent of the people you meet say, 'What a lovely job; can I come along and carry your bags?' The other fifty say, 'What's Jack Nicklaus really like?'

Many years ago, I developed an intense pain in one of my toes. I hobbled around to the doctor who happened to be a golf fanatic. 'Hello,' he said. 'Have a seat. Tell me, what's Jack Nicklaus really like?' I slipped off my shoe and clasped my throbbing foot with an expression of extreme anguish. He said, 'On TV he comes across as being a bit dour.' I conceded that Jack could be dour on occasion. The effort of resisting the agony made me burst out in perspiration. Twenty minutes later, after we had gone through Barbara being a wonderful mother and supportive wife, Jackie a chip off the old block, Stevie looking like being the better golfer, Nan getting engaged to her roommate's brother and Michael being a right little tearaway, he said, 'Something wrong with your foot? I daresay it's gout,' and wrote me out a prescription for butazoladine. That's the stuff you are forbidden to give horses.

I kept going back for fourteen years. It was the same routine every time. 'What's Lee Trevino really like?' Twenty minutes later, he would say, 'Toe still playing you up, is it? Here's some stuff a traveller left. Let me know if it does any good.' Eventually, I had a particularly virulent attack but my doctor was away on holiday and I had to see a locum. He looked through my notes and asked, 'What makes you think you've got gout?'

He sent me for a test and it proved negative. I had the toe amputated. It seemed the only solution.

You will understand if I do not talk to you about golfers. Most of them are extremely tedious people anyway, not nearly as interesting as the people with whom I shared a working lifetime of leaky press tents, a million miles of boring air travel, fierce competition for first use of the only telephone, ditto the port-a-loo, and endless hours propping up bars.

I barely knew Bernard Darwin when he was alive but after his death I got to know him extremely well by proxy, because Pat Ward-Thomas of the *Guardian* made it his life's work to become a reincarnation of Darwin. When his Wellington was shot down in one of the first raids over Germany, he was plain Flight-Lieutenant Percy Thomas. During four years in Stalag Luft 3, he acquired the hyphen, a new Christian name, a poetic literary style and a temper of truly Darwinian ferocity.

We called him the fireman because of his frenzied driving, and our instincts for self-preservation made us all extremely reluctant to let him into the driver's seat. At Augusta, they gave us a courtesy car and we quickly appointed Mark Wilson of the London *Evening Standard* as our official driver. On the very first journey, he demolished the gatepost of our rented house. Henry Longhurst growled, 'I have been in a number of road accidents but never one involving a teetotaller as the driver. I find this quite unforgiveable.'

Before we knew it, Pat Ward-Thomas had commandeered the keys. In fact, he did all right until the final day. The routine was that we left the cars at the airport and Pat was afraid there wasn't quite enough petrol left to get us there. We all chipped in a dollar and Pat drew into a filling station. He handed the money to the attendant and ordered five dollars worth. The attendant followed the usual routine of sticking the hose into the tank and then coming round to the front of the car to wash the windscreen. At the conclusion of this operation, he put down the wipers and Pat, assuming that he was now cleared for take off, drove on, tearing the hose from its pump. It took appliances from seventeen fire stations to neutralize the risk of a major explosion.

Leonard Crawley was a throwback to the golden age of amateur sports. He played golf up to the Amateur Championship, which was held in May in those days. He then switched to cricket as captain of Essex. One of his contemporaries said of Leonard that the only way to bowl at him was to let the ball go and duck for cover behind the umpire. In 1931, he had to make the agonizing choice between going to Australia with Douglas Jardine's test team or playing in the Walker Cup match in America. On August 12th, he put away his cricket bat in favour of his sporting guns, for he was one of the best shots in the country. He was therefore an honoured guest at some country house or shooting lodge for almost every week of the year.

But at the end of the war, which for Leonard was a continuation of his sporting life by other means, he was faced with having to earn his living, a considerable problem because he had no experience whatever of the harsh realities of life. His conception of journalism was that you wrote things down on something called an expense account and some office wallah would give you money. Accordingly, after his first overseas trip for the *Daily Telegraph*, across the Channel to play in the French Amateur Championship, he began his list of expenses with the item: 'To two tropical suits'.

His working methods were no less idiosyncratic. Reporting was a time consuming business which frequently clashed with his social arrangements. So, from time to time he would arrange to telephone some of his old Cambridge chums for information about what had happened at the golf and then write his report at some distant country house on the moors. The snag with this arrangement is that old Cambridge chums are prone to jolly japes, which is how the *Daily Telegraph* one year published a full account of an Amateur Championship final between two players who had actually been eliminated in the semi-finals.

It was the sublime writing of Longhurst which fired my enthusiasm for golf and it was his friendship, along with that of Leonard and Pat and Peter Ryde of *The Times*, that sustained me for thirty years or so. They have all gone except for the courtly and scholarly Peter Ryde, who we called the maniac-klepto because of his absent-minded habit of going into shops and leaving things.

I must turn to the business in hand. Ferndown, it seems to me, represents the very best of English golf. The very earth the club is built on is uniquely English. The slightly acid sands and gravels sustain the silver birch and gorse and heather and beech and pine and fine fescue grasses. These are the images of England which the homesick exile sees in his dreams. This English heathland is perfect for golf and Ferndown ranks high among our great heathland courses. As for the clubhouse and the club, there are doubtless those who find them slightly old fashioned. And all the better for that, say I, because they preserve the virtues and values of a more gracious age.

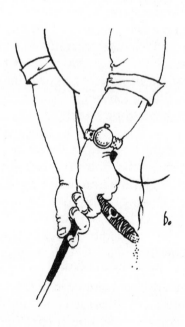

FIVE: ODDS 'n' SODS

Golf: the game that invented man.

Quote me a quote

Once upon a time, before you and I were born, it was the custom of newspapers to carry reports of sporting events. Our correspondent would go along to, say, a cricket match and describe what he saw. 'Grace dispatched the crimson orb to the confines for the full complement.' And much, much more in similar captivating style.

These days, readers are not interested in what a player did. They are fascinated to learn what a player said he did. Unless a sportsman can talk a good game he is nothing. I am old enough to remember when the craze of quote-journalism first fired the imagination of sports editors and, as a practitioner in the field, it was uphill work, I can tell you.

At a tournament in Yorkshire, Neil Coles and Bernard Hunt were playing together. Of course, being professionals, they were never favoured with the use of their Christian names, thereby becoming the source of frequent nightmares for the late Henry Longhurst, the pioneer TV commentator.

Coles and Hunt were professionals of the old school, brought up in the tradition that sportsmen should be seen and not heard. They simply could not take to this new-fangled idea of answering questions, and in those early interviews they responded mostly with embarrassed grunts. On this occasion, they had both scored well and were duly wheeled into the press tent to be grilled for the day's quotes. Hunt first. 'Drive, six, two putts. Drive, edge, two putts ...' The recital continued to the fourteenth hole. 'Drive, four, two putts.' At this point, Coles, who was just beginning to grasp the fundamentals of the new journalism, gave a faint cough and raised one eyebrow about a millimetre. Hunt stopped his recital and looked at Coles in bewilderment.

'Aren't you going to tell them about the fourteenth?' whispered Coles. 'The fourteenth?' said Hunt. 'Regulation par.' 'No,' hissed Coles. 'You know ...' Say what you like about us sports writers but we can sniff a story. 'What happened at the fourteenth?' we bayed. It was like drawing teeth, but we persisted and bit by bit it all came out. As he was addressing the ball for the approach shot, Hunt's club was struck from his hands by lightning.

Eventually, we had our story, justifying the new system, for it was almost as good as if we had seen the incident ourselves, although try as we might we couldn't get much of a quote out of Hunt. What did you do when lightning hit you? 'I picked up the club and hit the ball. Front left, about 20 feet.' Not the most arresting utterance you have heard, perhaps, but it was a start.

How times have changed. Ten years later, the players had mastered the art of the quote. When Lee Trevino was hit by lightning at the Western Open he did thirty minutes of stand-up comedy patter without drawing breath and he had a column of quotes in every newspaper. That is why he is a superstar.

These days, young professionals are taught the art of the quote at the American qualifying school and they have to sign a declaration agreeing to cooperate with the media at all times, meaning that they must be ready with a quotable quote at the drop of a tape recorder.

The most important time for quotes is before a tournament when the newspapers are obsessively devoting columns and columns to reports of what is going to happen. This is one of my favourite journalistic exercises and I live for the day when I master the art of prognostication to such a degree that it will not be necessary to report the actual event at all. I shall simply write: 'The Open Championship was played yesterday and turned out exactly as I forecast five days ago. Back numbers are available from the circulation department.'

Arnold Palmer is the absolute master of the quote and I cherish particularly his reply to a quote-hungry writer before the US Open Championship.

'Do you think the guys can shoot low on this course, Arnie?'

'Waaall, any time you drive the ball in the fairway, hit all the greens and make a bunch of putts then you have a chance to make a good score.'

When professionals are talking about their own play, their remarks can only be properly understood if you happen to know their scores. I have therefore invented a new form of punctuation which I hope will be universally adopted by newspapers for golfing quotes. Here is how it works.

Jerry Pate led the first round and said: 63 I really enjoyed playing this superb course which has been beautifully prepared for the championship. 63

Or. Larry Nelson commented: 75 They could do with lowering the cutters of the fairway mowers; I had a lot of flyers. 75

Or. Lanny Wadkins snarled: 82 I'd like to get hold of the clown who set those pin positions and give him a lobotomy – with my wedge. 82

By now, we experienced hands, both players and writers, have refined the quotes business to a fine art. I glance at the scoreboard and notice that David Graham, for instance, has been posted with a score of 76. A few years ago, this would have required a complicated ritual involving a tape recorder and laborious transcription, followed by the editing out of any fruity adjectives and then the writing of the rough draft. Now, under the mutual trust system, the process can be streamlined.

Self: 'How?'

Graham: 'Tripled five.'

I can now go straight to the typewriter and begin: 'David

Graham's challenge faltered with a third-round 76. An otherwise solid performance was marred by a torrid seven at the innocuous 370-yard fifth hole, where the players enjoyed the help of a light following breeze. Graham reeled from the course ashen faced and groaned, 'I played that hole like an arthritic granny.'

You may purse your lips and mutter about a decline in journalistic ethics but it is necessary to invent quotes more and more these days because professional golfers are gradually losing the power of speech. Already adverbs have been eliminated entirely from their vocabulary. 'I hit the ball super but putted just horrible.' Some of these semantic murderers have gone further and limit themselves to the use of one adjective only, employing it on every possible occasion and sometimes in the middle of a word, thus: 'I played a low com-****-pression ball.'

These developments in the world of golf reporting have transformed our lives. We cannot waste time enjoying the sunshine and fresh air on the golf course because hard necessity requires us to produce quotes. For reasons which I have explained, we mostly have to invent such quotes, putting a gigantic strain on the imagination. The only way this can be achieved successfully, day after day, is by the use of artificial stimulants. Greatly against my natural inclinations, and indeed to my abhorrence, I myself have occasionally to resort to the use of hallucinatory drugs, of which alcohol is the only form available in golf clubs. So, if you should happen to see a golf writer in the bar while a tournament is in progress, please suppress that unfortunately common instinct to remark sneeringly, 'I thought you reporter chappies were paid to watch golf.'

We are sensitive to such ignorant jibes. Just remember that as we force ourselves to swallow that hateful amber fluid through clenched teeth we are actually performing a difficult and distasteful task for *your benefit* and in order to support our families.

> *Despite this column, it could never be said of Peter that his writing was largely sustained by quotes.*

(GOLF WORLD 1979)

An eagle at the seventh.

All in the mind

How do you feel when you hear a professional golfer announce that he simply must take a break for a month or so because he has played for three straight weeks?

I can scarce forebear to burst into tears of sympathy for the poor chap. How incredibly sad in this age of enlightenment that any human being should have to endure three solid weeks of living in five-star hotels, being ferried about in courtesy limousines, playing a leisurely eighteen holes a day and getting paid obscenely extravagant amounts of money for it all.

Just imagine the scene 2,000 feet below ground in the Welsh valleys where Taffy Jones, cramped in a two-foot seam, is hacking at the coal face with his pick, soaked in his own sweat and urine in the foetid heat.

'Why are you sobbing, Taff?'

'I was just thinking about those poor bloody golfers having to play three, even four weeks in a row before they can take off for a month's fishing. It's the sheer inhumanity of it. I can't help myself crying when I think about the affront to the dignity of man to have to earn a living in those appalling conditions.'

Yes, yes, I know that it is the mental strain of playing top-level competitive golf that makes it necessary for the superstars to take off for Barbados at frequent intervals. The reason I know is that I was present for the press interview by Severiano Ballesteros when he railed at the assembled company that we did not know, that we could never know, the pressures involved in championship golf.

I glanced around the room and identified among my col-

leagues a commando who had survived the Normandy bea-
ches, two wartime pilots, one RAF, one Navy, another RAF
man, a guardsman who had been right through the desert
campaign in World War II and a retired professional boxing
champion. The irony of the situation prompted a moment of
idle speculation about whether the historian, Sir Walter Simpson, might not have had a point when he wrote that excessive
golfing dwarfs the intellect.

He went further and suggested that a stunted intellect was a
prerequisite for good golf, saying in *The Art of Golf*, published
in 1892 'the more fatuously vacant the mind is, the better for
play. It has been observed that absolute idiots ... play stead-
iest. An uphill game does not make them press, nor victory
within their grasp render them careless. Alas! We cannot all be
idiots. Next to the idiotic, the dull unimaginative mind is best
for golf. In a professional competition I would prefer to back
the sallow, dull-eyed fellow with a "quid" in his cheek, rather
than any more eager-looking fellow.'

I would take issue with Sir Walter when he bemoans the fact
that we cannot all be idiots. For myself, I have no problems at
all in turning into a raving halfwit on the golf course. And I
have observed that many great statesmen and mandarins of
industry have this same faculty. Indeed, what sets the professional apart from the amateur, far more than any disparity
in skill, is the pro's ability to retain his sanity while playing this
daft game.

But is it true that the golfer who is as thick as two planks has
an advantage over rivals who are less intellectually challenged? The evidence is by no means conclusive.

Bobby Jones was an intellectual giant as well as being my
nominee for the greatest golfer of all time. Furthermore, he had
a highly imaginative and creative mind, thereby challenging
another of Simpson's conclusions: 'The poetic temperament is
the worst for golf.'

Peter Thomson is a polymath who, one feels, could have
succeeded at whatever he set his mind to, hence the pressures

put upon him to go into politics. The fact that he did not pursue this course simply endorses the high intelligence of the man. Tom Watson, who tied Thomson's five Open Championships, probably equals him also in weight and quality of grey matter.

Jack Nicklaus would wince and snort with indignation if you described him as an intellectual, but the reason he became the most succesful golfer in the history of the game owed as much, or more, to a well-disciplined mind as a good swing.

No doubt there are plenty of golfers in the current top 100 of the world rankings who do not have to be reminded by their caddies to put up their umbrellas when it rains. But there are some players today who think PR simply represents the first two letters in prat; who clearly believe that they do not need the newspapers, radio or television any more.

That is a rash assumption. And those who have declared war against the communicators should think again, because they are embarked on a suicide mission.

Anyone who thinks he can win such a war simply proves Sir Walter's point.

(GOLF WORLD 1992)

Terrors of the pro-am

Everybody knows that the greatest glory of the game of golf is a handicapping system that enables the veriest rabbit to play on level terms with Jack Nicklaus. Everybody who has actually put this glory to the test knows it to be a load of cobblers.

However, since there is only one Jack Nicklaus and at a rough count there are some 30–40 million rabbits, the myth survives and there is never any shortage of romantic fools who believe that their handicap strokes make them the equal of the star tournament players.

Hence the pro-am, a highly refined form of golf torture whose only merit is that it raises millions and millions of pounds for charity every year.

A non-golfer with a keen grasp of higher mathematics will tell you that the handicap system is foolproof. A 16-handicapper will, by definition, play sixteen strokes more than par and, if he gets his full stroke allowance, as mostly happens in pro-ams, he will have a 72, which is likely to be the score of his pro.

In practice, it does not work like that. What happens is that as soon as the 16-handicapper learns that he has been drawn to play with Sandy Lyle he breaks into a cold sweat. Strictly speaking, he is clinically mad from now on with a mental derangement known to psychiatrists as Toad of Toad Hall Syndrome. The syndrome includes severe dislocation from reality, fantasies about playing a career best round of 73, less 16, giving a net 57, probably followed by a request from the admiring Lyle to come to the practice ground and pass on a few tips.

The disease now follows a predictable pattern. The victim goes to the pro's shop and splurges on a new colour co-ordinated outfit of shirt, sweater, slacks, glove, cap, pro bag and, the first fatal error, new shoes. The second really disastrous mistake is that he also books up for a lesson. Having guaranteed that he will suffer from blistered heels and that his limited ability will have deteriorated by a minimum of ten strokes a round, he is now ready for the big day.

When they meet on the first tee, Lyle could not be more comforting. 'Just play your normal game and don't worry about anything. We'll have a nice, friendly round.' Our poor booby tries to reply but owing to the dryness of his throat his merry quip comes out as a Donald Duck croak. There are, he estimates, some 10,000 spectators gathered around the first tee, all of them wearing expressions of mocking amusement.

Something very peculiar is happening to his knees. His name is called and he tees his ball. A sudden spasm afflicts his hands and the ball falls off the tee. Someone in the gallery titters. By the time he straightens up, his hands are trembling uncontrollably, a problem for which there is only one solution. He grasps the driver in a grip so tight that all circulation of blood below the wrist is thwarted. It has to go somewhere and, as he addresses the ball, a red glaze covers his eyes, effectively blinding him. His rising panic is compounded by the sudden realization that he has forgotten what he is supposed to do with the golf club. Some vestigial instinct prompts him to raise the driver in the manner of a drunken executioner lifting his sword; in a convulsive spasm he brings it down again. The toe of the driver catches the ball a glancing blow, causing it to shoot off at a right angle and inflict painful shin wounds among the sneering populace.

That tangential cover drive from the first tee is a common opening gambit in pro-ams, but there are several interesting variations: the air shot, the scuttling squirt into the left rough, the swing which passes clean underneath the ball in a flurry of flying turf and tee peg, leaving the ball to drop vertically into the crater. My own speciality used to be the premature evacuation, with the club-head entering the turf 11 inches (my personal best) behind the ball and ploughing onwards with a growing accumulation of grass and dirt pushed by my impromptu bulldozer blade just far enough to topple the ball from its peg.

Renton Laidlaw of the London *Evening Standard* pioneered an elegant variation on this gambit, his club-head stopping two inches short of its target, having neatly curled a divot right over the ball which sat there undisturbed beneath its leafy canopy. (He then uncurled the divot, stamped it flat and hit a whizzer down the fairway, although I have always maintained that he should have penalized himself for improving his lie.)

Anyway, once the pantomime of the opening tee shot is over, things tend to improve and, speaking of penalties, the pro-am amateur should lose no opportunity to pull the integrity ploy. Once you are sure your score cannot contribute to the team's fortunes, call a penalty on yourself, whether or not it is justified, ostentatiously put your ball away and announce: 'I'm afraid you chaps will have to do the business on this hole. Damn ball moved at the address.' You thus create the impression of honest endeavour thwarted by bad luck and, incidentally, contribute to the speed of play.

If you are of a certain age, you can further salvage your esteem within the group by steering the conversation around to the war. Inevitably, someone will mention an item of military hardware, such as the Scharnhorst or the Tiger or the Junkers 87. That's your opening. You snort: 'Don't talk to me about Stukas; I've spent the last forty years trying to forget the damn things.' Then you walk quickly away, trying hard not to limp.

By such conversational strategies the experienced pro-am hand can contribute not a single point to the team's welfare but win the reputation as a frightfully decent chap, brave, modest and cheerful even though he was dreadfully unlucky with the golf. Obviously, a pretty useful player, but it was just not his day.

The identity of the professional introduces an element of lottery into pro-ams. If you can afford it, the best plan is to bribe the officials to team you with the pro of your choice. Otherwise, the day can be a disaster. I once had to play with an Italian assistant and two amateurs of the same nationality, not one of whom spoke a word of English, nor, as far as I could judge, had a passing acquaintance with the laws of the game. At the other end of the scale, the best pro by far was Max Faulkner who kept us in enthralled hysterics with ribald anecdotes about famous players. He also gave the impression that the sole purpose of the day was to cure our faults and he gave us each a lesson before every shot. His own golf was purely incidental. 'I'll just give this a swish.' By the end, we were all hitting the ball quite respectably. I think he scored a 67.

Tommy Horton and Brian Barnes are inheritors of this tradition but not every pro is quite so amenable. That is understandable. Just imagine that you have missed four cuts in a row, the bank manager is making hostile noises and, owing to a mechanical failure of your car, it's your only chance to study and pace the course before the tournament. You explain all this before the round and crave the indulgence of your amateurs, promising to chat as much as they like between holes. Off you go, measuring the distance to the front of the green: 176, 177, 178, 179 –

'I say, pro, what's Arnold Palmer really like?'

'Eh?'

'I mean, he comes across as a nice guy on TV but I wondered if that was all a front.'

'No, he is a nice guy. Excuse me a minute, I'm counting out my yardage. Now, where the hell was I? 205, 206, 207 . . .'

Most pros have a litany of automatic responses which they can utter without breaking their train of thought. The sound of club-head making solid contact with a ball prompts the reflex

'Hey! Who's the pro in this group?' as automatically as a 'pardon' after a belch. Bernard Gallacher, bless him, has developed a brilliant strategy. Every time an amateur asks, 'What club should I take?' Gallacher answers, '3-wood,' even if the ball is on the fringe of the green. The beauty of that system is that it absolves him of all necessity for thought and his advice always results in a satisfactory shot.

The real pleasure of pro-ams is not to be found in showing off your golfing talent but in being able to observe at close quarters the extraordinary skills of the pro. And if you can persuade him to show off, especially if he is a magician like Severiano Ballesteros, the participation in a pro-am becomes the golfing experience of the amateur's life.

The other lasting satisfaction of participating in pro-ams comes later, when you are back at the club with a lifetime's ammunition for boring the pants off your friends. 'I shall never forget when I was playing with Queenie, that's what all his friends call Michael King, and he said that with my swing if I could devote an hour a day to my golf I could get down to scratch in six months . . .'

(GOLF WORLD 1983)

Golf – the game that invented man

Scientists who search for the origin of man work to a time-honoured formula. The newly graduated anthropologist departs for East Africa and spends twenty years grubbing around in the dirt with a trowel until finally, with a Neanderthal grunt of triumph, he rises to his feet holding a minute splinter of fossilized shinbone.

This he carefully traces on a large sheet of paper and then, from his vast knowledge and experience, he outlines with a dotted line the silhouette of the creature that originally owned that bit of bone. Invariably, this reconstruction turns out to resemble a naked golfer strolling down a fairway.

The scientist now has to ask himself the vital question: Was this creature a man or an ape? There are certain standard tests to determine the answer. Did it possess the power of reason? Did it communicate by speech? Did it have a sense of humour?

My own brilliant contribution to this scientific discipline has been to devise a vastly simplified system of distinguishing man from ape. All the scientist has to do is ask one straightforward question: Could this creature have played golf?

You can perhaps guess the line of research that I am now pursuing. Most scientists accept that the origin of our species occurred along the pattern laid down by Charles Darwin, namely that some time, for some reason, an ape decided to stand on his back legs and walk erect, thereby becoming a man.

That is fine as far as it goes, but the theory begs the central question of why an ape should suddenly decide to stand up. I am a committed Darwinian but I prefer Bernard to Charles. My theory is that there was only one possible reason for an ape to stand up on his hind legs: to play golf.

Imagine our original ancestor, when in his ape form, moving on all fours along a jungle track. A small armadillo runs out and stops in terror, rolling itself into a perfect sphere for protection. The ape, equally taken aback, grabs a stick and whacks at the creature. The armadillo describes a perfect parabola through the air, lands on a grassy glade, takes two hops forward and then checks under the influence of backspin and rolls slowly into a rabbit hole.

Another ape, witnessing this scene, snatches the wretched armadillo from the hole, grabs the stick and tries to emulate that remarkable ace. The ape family is notorious for its penchant for imitation; it would be irresistible for the second ape. Thus, golf was born.

Now, with the rudimentary game established, the way was open for the birth of mankind and the dawn of civilization. The apes had to learn to walk upright. They also had to learn how to fashion golf clubs, variations of which were used for hunting. The power of reason developed with succeeding generations so that these primitive golfers could decide on club selection, read borrows in the greens and work out the bets.

As night follows day, those first men would have had to devise a means of spoken communication, if only to tell each other lies about how they would have broken 70 had a passing brontosaurus not deflected the ball on the last green. So *Homo erectus* became *Homo sapiens* and the way was cleared for man to conquer the earth and, in due course, the heavens. We have golf to thank for Shakespeare's sonnets and Rembrandt's portraits.

However, if we observe life in a cosmic context, we see that everything goes in cycles. Plants emerge in spring, flourish and wither in the fall, then lie dormant before the process begins again. We humans are born, struggle to get down to single-figure handicaps and then return to the earth, which gave us our being. We tend to accept that the civilizing process of man will continue forever, in a steadily rising graph of progress. Be warned. There is evidence to suggest that the process that produced man from ape is itself a cycle. The process of decay is evident in the same sphere that started it all: golf.

Let us go back to those original definitions of man and see how our modern pro golfers measure up.

The power of reason: Apart from Jack Nicklaus, and to a lesser degree Tom Watson, this faculty seems to be disappearing.

Sense of humour: Totally vanished from the world of golf except for Lee Trevino.

Ability to speak: Here we have the hard evidence. 'I played super but putted mediocre.' That is the standard response of golfers today. The adverb has vanished from the vocabulary of golf. Other parts of speech are falling into disuse, as in the expression, 'I tripled five.'

On the golf course, the players communicate in grunts. In the space of eighteen holes a player may utter no more than half a dozen words: 'Yer up.' 'Short.' 'I'll finish.' 'Joyed it.'

I do not know whether it is possible to arrest this regression to the cave age, but I do feel we should try. Unless something is done – and quickly – it seems that by the next century man will drop down onto all fours again. And, quite possibly, start growing a tail.

(GOLF WORLD 1982)

Sheer self-denial

There was no collusion, I promise, although it would not have made any difference. As a veteran of a thousand editorial conferences I am all too familiar with the way a bad idea can germinate and flourish on a thin news day:

'As chroniclers and devotees of sport, we ought to be setting an example in the ongoing *mens sana in corpore sano* situation. I think it would make a deeply meaningful exercise if we sent one man swanning off to a health farm for a week. At this time of year they are mostly filled with strippers toning up for the cabaret season. McIlvanney would be perfect. Then, we could send Brasher to run up and down Scandinavia. Now, all we need is someone to go on a bread and water diet.'

It could have happened like that, but it didn't. It was purely by coincidence that I decided my too, too solid flesh must be made to melt. 'Terrific,' they said. 'Write five hundred words about how you did it.' Very well, here goes.

I have not eaten for forty-eight days.

That's seven words and that is about all there was to it. Actually, it started on the golf course. There is a steep rise between the second green and third tee at my club and, while I did not deliberately lose that second hole, I found myself grateful not to have the honour on the third because that gave me a chance to catch my breath.

My weight had never bothered me much before. What is $16\frac{1}{2}$ stone, after all? 'You've got the height to carry it,' friends assured me. Fat people have a remarkable capacity for finding virtues in fatness. Physical solidarity is equated with moral dependability. What rot. Yon Cassius has a lean and hungry look. Give me men around me who have a low cholesterol level in their blood.

I made a number of firm decisions. I would not go on a diet. I would not become a Weight-Watcher. I would not slim. That would be antisocial, for there is no bore quite so boring as a slimming bore, lest it be a fitness freak, than whom no other variety of bore can bore your tits off more rapidly. Much as I wished to lose my own pendulous paps, I would not eliminate them at the expense of other people's. I began by shaving off my beard and moustache; an important psychological step this, for it instantly transformed me into a different person, which was the object of the exercise. Then, I stopped eating. It was not total self-denial, you understand. But where I would have taken ten mouthfuls before, I cut my consumption down to one. By the time the novelty of a shaven chin had worn off, so had a gratifying stone or so of excess blubber.

I took to not wearing a hat, since 60 per cent of the body's heat loss is through the head (or so I had read somewhere), and I thought that my metabolism would have to dig deeply into the reserve supplies of fat in order to maintain normal body temperature. It does not work out like that. Just as women's thighs grew thicker in the mini skirt era, so my scalp seemed to develop a protective layer of lard. End of experiment.

The crisis in every weight-reducing regime is the moment when the bathroom scales seem to stick. You are still not eating, but you are not losing any more fat. Some days you actually go up a bit. Up till now, I had not thought about calories, but I fell into slimming-bore ways to counter my depression. As a result, the daily half bottle of claret was struck off the programme, to be replaced for social purposes by slim-line tonic with a dash of lime. The odd slice of bread, I discovered, was not too high calorically. The real poison is the butter and the cheese. By converting my boilers to black tea and coffee, with sweeteners instead of sugar, and to hell with the scare about cyclamates, I got the weighing machine needle on the move again.

After a bit, my appetite began to shrink in direct ratio to my diminishing waistline, and that is half the battle. Losing weight is all very well but unless you stay slim – and that means changing your eating habits – then the exercise is a waste of time and willpower.

Numerous benefits flowed from my weeks of self-denial, such as a ten-year-old suit which not only fits again but is almost back in fashion. I cannot say that I ever suffered greatly from flatulence (truth to tell I rather enjoyed it), but there has been a dramatic drop in turbulence. My golf has improved by a good six shots a round.

Was it worth it? Certainly, both physically and mentally I am a different person. Of course, I am still a slob, but a thin slob, and there is a world of difference between the two.

A kind of throwback to the TW3-type material, it reflects man's frustrating search for a better figure, on the course or on the scales.

(OBSERVER 1978)

Golfers on a short fuse

So far as we know, golf grew to popularity on the east coast of Scotland round about the year 1430 and so it is safe to assume that by 1450 people were going round shaking their heads in a nostalgic manner and complaining, 'There aren't any characters in the game any more.' Certainly by the end of the century, the phrase was well established in the litany of golf, along with 'Never up, never in' and 'Golf is a humbling game'.

It was not true then and it is not true now and it will never be true so long as the human character is spiced with the ingredient called temper. Younger readers may be unfamiliar with the monologues of Marriott Edgar, and it is their loss, but that wonderful Lancashire music-hall performer wrote an ode which exactly traces the emotional sequence of my favourite golf incident. The poem starts:

Joe Ramsbottom rented a bit of a farm
From its owner, Squire Goslett his name;
And the Gosletts came over with William the First,
And found Ramsbottoms here when they came.

The event described in this ditty was that Joe broke the coulter on his plough, decided that it would save time if he borrowed a spare one from the nearby Squire's farm, felt that such a request might be presumptuous, berated himself for his diffidence since it was the Squire's rock which had busted his plough, assured himself that he was as good as any stuck-up Squire and, having received a friendly greeting at the front door, let fly with the final verse:

> Then he said 'P'raps you think yourself better than me
> Well, I'm telling you straight that you're not,
> And I don't want your coulter, your plough or your farm,
> You can – do what you like with the lot.'

Clayton Heafner was a pretty fair golfer and a spiritual brother of Joe Ramsbottom. Driving to one tournament, Clayton began to reflect on his last visit to this club and how he had had to climb a tree to dislodge his ball, no paltry feat for a man of his bulk. This and sundry other memories mingled with the yeast of his temper and by the time he drove into the club's car park the fermentation was bubbling dangerously. He stopped the car, yelled 'You can keep your goddamn trees and your whole goddamn golf course!' and drove off again.

Another American of that pre-war era, Lefty Stackhouse, was also a slow boiler. He made valiant efforts to keep himself in control and might finish his round with complete decorum, but experienced Stackhouse watchers knew that there was a formidable head of pressure within his powerful frame and waited for the delayed reaction. Suddenly, he would explode, breaking all his clubs or, on one occasion, systematically demolishing his roadster in the car park. On balance, it was probably preferable when he got it out of his system there and then, which he did by punching himself on the jaw or kicking himself in the leg. Lefty was a pretty keen and pretty regular performer with the bottle and one day, in his woozy condition, he laid himself out cold on the golf course with a right hook.

The commonest form of golfing outrage takes the form of uncontrolled hatred for the equipment of the game, mostly the putter. In his youth our own Mark James, today a golfer of impeccable deportment, went through a phase of marked antipathy towards his feckless putter. Their relationship deteriorated to such a degree during the Bob Hope Benefit Classic, or whatever it was called, at the RAC Country Club, Epsom, that he kicked the horrible curse of disappointment as he took the putter back. But Tommy Bolt was the most famous exponent of the popping cork and even wrote instructional articles on the art, advocating such policies as making sure that you throw the club forward. Saves the legs.

Apart from throwing and breaking clubs, Bolt also had a lurid vocabulary and his expletives sometimes reached the ears of the gallery. That would never do and the American PGA instituted a system of fines to curb his tongue, $100 per cuss word. A monitor was appointed to follow Bolt around the course and keep tally of his language. At the end of the round, the committee sent for Bolt and fined him $200. He paid up and went to the bar, where his fellow pros were surprised to see him sipping his drink and smiling like a cat which had swallowed the canary. Since his demeanour suggested that it was safe to approach him, a player observed that he looked remarkably cheerful considering that they had just fined him $200. 'Yes,' said Bolt smugly, 'but I stiffed the bastards for 1,500 bucks.'

(OBSERVER 1984)

Wanted: a new Messiah

Opinions in golf go in fashions. Do you remember the late-hit craze? Somebody, probably Ben Hogan although I am open to correction, said that the late hit was what separated the pros from the amateurs. Millions of golfers tried to master the secret of the late hit without knowing what it meant or, to be precise, without realizing that the expression was meaningless. The whole thing blew up into prominence because cameras of the day distorted the mechanics of the swing, and then a new craze came along and everybody forgot about trying to hit late.

Then, there was the business of 'drive for show and putt for dough'. That had a ring to it and seemed, like 'Never up, never in', to encapsulate an essential truth. It took some of us years to shake those gems of wisdom from our minds and see them for what they were, trite to the point of banality. Willie Park's famous battle cry: 'The man who can putt is a match for anyone', is another example of golfing booby-talk which had a considerable vogue.

Now I believe we are in for another glib and questionable generalization. These days, tournament golfers are subjected to the compulsory interview after any round lower than 72. Being taken into the pressroom has become a ritual and a small reward, less than a medal but a commendation in the form of a warm beer and a mention in the papers. The ritual aspect of the interview involves a shot-by-shot recital of the round. The old hands get through their litany at high speed, like a vicar at a thinly congregated Evensong when there is steak for dinner.

'First: drive, 4-iron, two putts. Second: 5-iron, 20-footer . . .'

The novices stumble and forget their clubbing and the holes.

'What's that par-five on the front?' Well-organized writers who have furnished themselves with a card of the course supply the hole number. 'Well, I came off my tee shot and wound up in the right rough.' 'What club?' 'Driver – no, I took my 3-wood.'

Being dutiful servants of our readers, we take copious notes. Besides, it would be impolite to just sit there yawning. (As soon as the player has left the room we throw away these notes on the grounds that they make duller reading than the London telephone directory.) What we want is electrifying copy, preferably involving stark human drama, incredible hardships, violence, hard drugs, big money or sex, preferably all of them. Since professional golfers are mainly level-headed, clean-living young men, we are mostly disappointed, but we keep probing for a quotable quote. What we are getting more and more these days is the opinion that the day of the superstar is over. 'The depth of the tour is now so strong that anybody can win any week. Not so long ago there were perhaps ten or twenty players in the field who were capable of winning but nowadays every guy who makes the cut is a potential winner.'

Goodness knows who started this notion. I suspect that it was a line dreamed up by a backroom publicist of the American tour to promote the idea that golf has produced a race of supermen of uniform excellence and to blur the fact that Jack Nicklaus, Arnold Palmer and Gary Player are getting a bit long in the tooth and can no longer do the business week after week.

Sophistry is dangerous stuff because it is essentially plausible. It is self-evident that any professional can win any tournament in theory. Further, you can back up that claim with 'proof' by listing some recent unlikely tournament winners, provided you omit the relevant fact that the tournaments in question did not attract the presence of the full complement of established stars. You might as well argue that because I have a typewriter and a supply of paper there is nothing to stop me from walking away with the Nobel prize for literature. Keep about a million good writers out of the contest and I might stand a chance.

The day of the superstar, I am convinced, is far from over. Lee Trevino recently gave a frank appraisal of his contemporary superstars in support of his theme that all of them had weaknesses. Nicklaus lacked a short game; Severiano Ballesteros was inconsistent with the driver; Bill Rogers was so slightly built that he did not have the strength and stamina for sustained golf; Tom Watson had only one speed, full ahead. He could not play a soft shot. Gary Player suffered from a hook. As for himself, Trevino was handicapped by a lack of length. 'The Lord,' he said, 'does not give anyone everything. He always holds back something.'

Nobody would quarrel with Trevino's assessments, but I suspect that his conclusion that every person is flawed by divine intention will be challenged by theologians and golfers alike. Why on earth or, indeed, in heaven should there not be a golfer who has everything? Bobby Jones came close to being the ideal all-round golfer with no obvious weaknesses. Byron Nelson tamed the game of golf, briefly but gloriously. Henry Cotton, Ben Hogan and Harry Vardon had just about everything except for consistent putting strokes.

As for the bleak appraisal that the day of the superstar is past for ever, I reject it totally. There will be new superstars and the odds are that one of them will surpass anything we have yet seen in golf. I just hope that I am around to watch him.

Today, of course, we have Tiger Woods. Sadly, Peter was 'not around to watch him'. Tiger turned turned pro within a month of Peter's passing. Although Peter did, of course, see Ernie Els.

(OBSERVER 1982)

Dressing to kill

A British golfer will not win the Open. I am sorry about that, for we have a few potential champions around and a British victory would do wonders for the game. However, it is impossible.

Shallow-minded critics have complained for years that British golfers are lazy, unambitious and unwilling to make the sacrifices which are necessary to pluck the game's richest plums. I have always felt that such arguments were specious, although I could not put my finger on the real reason for overseas domination of our championship.

Finally, I have discovered the underlying cause of British failure and I have been kicking myself unmercifully for my blindness.

Now, after full research and acute observations, I am able to state categorically that it has been impossible for a British player to win the Open since 1967. (Hairsplitting pedants may demur at this assertion and point out that Tony Jacklin won the Open in 1969. So he did, but if you will bear with me a little longer you will realize that Jacklin's victory was actually an American triumph. We have to go back to Max Faulkner's win in the 1951 Open to find the last true roast-beef- and-Yorkshire-pudding British Open champion.)

The blinding flash of revelation which laid bare the secret of overseas domination in recent Opens came to me at the Dunlop Masters when Jose Maria Canizares covered the front nine of the Duke's Course at Woburn in 29 strokes. Naturally, that performance recalled his remarkable feat of bagging eleven birdies and an eagle in unbroken succession during the Swiss Open at Crans-sur-Sierre.

From there, my train of thought naturally turned to Baldovino Dassu's score of 60 in the Swiss Open. The scene came back to me in vivid detail, with Dassu picking his ball out of the cup at the end of that historic round. As he bent down his fashionable trousers split asunder. That was it! I rushed to my reference books and checked the list of recent Open winners. Player, Jacklin, Nicklaus, Trevino, Weiskopf, Watson, Miller, Ballesteros. Different shapes, different sizes, different nationalities – but they had one common denominator: all of them wore quite remarkably tight trousers!

Now, think about the British players who might have won those championships judged purely on talent. John Panton, Neil Coles, Christy O'Connor, Bernard Hunt . . . gifted players, experienced players, but in the trousering department . . . ?

The effect of tight trousers is virtually to cut off blood supplies below the waist and that in turn means that the upper body gets double the usual ration of red corpuscles, oxygen, hormones, adrenalin and upper cylinder lubricant. The nervous system, with only half its usual territory to cover, is twice as effective, making the hands doubly sensitive and the brain doubly active. How can British golfers hope to compete against such supercharged players? Faulkner did it quite by accident because he wore plus fours and therefore had to wear tight bindings or garters below the knees to keep his stockings up. Jacklin, as you will recall, was a regular competitor on the American tour at the time of his victory at Lytham and so his wardrobe was American.

My findings throw considerable illumination on the history of competitive golf. Harry Vardon (six Opens) wore plus fours. So did Bobby Locke (four Opens). Locke never wore plus fours again after his victory at St Andrews in 1957. That was a private gesture of grateful tribute to the enlightened action of the championship committee in waiving any penalty for the technical offence of failing to replace his ball on the precise spot on the last green, but, significantly, once he took to wearing baggy trousers and his heart had to handle all the wasteful effort of pumping supplies right down to his toes and back again, he never won another championship.

Walter Hagen, who was rather a vain man over his appearance, wore his belt very tight in order to present his athletic figure to best advantage. Come to think of it, Peter Thomson also had an hourglass figure on the course and he must have pulled his belt in a notch or two. Arnold Palmer is a bit of a mystery because he won a few championships and his trousers were in constant danger of falling down. He was forever hitching them up and the only explanation I can offer for his success is that he must have worn very tight underpants. I must ask him about that some day.

We have our tradition of fine tailoring in Britain, with standards of fit and comfort laid down by the high priests of Savile Row. Surely we cannot sacrifice all that for the sake of boasting a home-grown Open champion? For mark my words, if our British sporting heroes switch to tight trousers, then the manufacturers will jump on the bandwagon and tight trousers will be all there is to buy in the shops. For myself, I am not prepared to endure the discomfort, which is why I am wary of that Nick Faldo. He is showing a distressing tendency to flout our baggy traditions and is compressing his extremeties into some fancy nether integuments these days. If he wins at Sandwich, I shall switch to a kilt.

Nick Faldo did not win the 1985 Open Championship at Sandwich. But a Brit did, and it was a traditionally kilt-wearing one – Sandy Lyle.

(GOLF WORLD 1984)

SIX: MAJOR GOLF

Down goes a barrier

When Lee Elder sank a long birdie putt at the fourth extra hole of a sudden-death play-off with Peter Oosterhuis in the Monsanto Open (1974), he won the first American PGA tournament of his career and thus became the first black golfer to qualify for an automatic invitation to compete in the Masters. I know only too well what relief that fact will bring to the tournament organizers at Augusta.

For years, the Masters has been reviled in certain quarters, notably among opportunist politicians looking to pick up black votes, as a bastion of southern bigotry. The tournament committee has answered these smears with long-suffering grace.

In the case of American golfers, invitations to play in the Masters are given in accordance with a set of fixed conditions, one of which is the winning of a PGA tour event during the previous year. The Masters has always stood out against tokenism, believing that if a special case were made to include a black golfer in the field, outside the limits of the qualifying standards, this would be seen as a patronizing act and would actually harm race relations.

For as long as I have been going to the Masters, the chairman, Clifford Roberts, whose word has been law for the forty years since the tournament began, has been questioned on this subject and he has always insisted, 'As soon as a black golfer becomes eligible for an invitation under the qualifying system, he will be welcome at Augusta just like anyone else.'

American professional golf has been integrated (by PGA rule) for many years, and this has been accepted by everyone in

the game as fully as in baseball, football or jazz music, for a
lesser period of time. If black golfers have been slow to come to
the top, the reasons must be sought in the wider American
society rather than within the game.

It was a pity that the last ritual of integration should not fall
to one of the men whose example over many years was mainly
responsible for dissolving prejudice. Ted Rhodes, reputedly
good enough to beat any white golfer of his day if only he had
been allowed to compete, and also Charlie Sifford, were both
born too early to claim the honour of this last act of emancipa-
tion, although Sifford still plays fine golf on occasions.

But Elder himself has borne a fair share of the pioneers'
burden. He will be forty in a few months, yet he did not join the
PGA circuit until 1968. Before then, he competed on the (black)
United Golf Association tour, contemptuously known as the
peanut circuit for its $1000 prizes. In that league, he was king,
once winning twenty-one out of the season's twenty-three
events, and earning enough to put by a nest egg which would
see him over the transition to the PGA big-time.

He is deeply committed to civil rights, not in the crusading
Arthur Ashe manner but as a visitor to underprivileged areas
where he encourages the children to remain in school and
elevate themselves educationally.

He himself dropped out, added a couple of years to his age
to comply with UGA regulations, and started playing pro golf
at fourteen.

Like many youngsters, Elder gripped his clubs cross-handed
until he went to work with Lloyd Mangrum, but he did not
really become serious about golf until he finished his stint in
the army. Mangrum helped him find a job as an assistant and
Elder, whose truck-driver father died when he was young,
supplemented the meagre family finances with a series of
hustling side bets. Elder would take on challenges to play on
one leg, on his knees and once, in 95° in a zipped-up rain
suit.

Elder did not go into these matches unprepared. Having

made the bet, he would go to a floodlit driving range to practise, sometimes working away all night and going straight to the match with no sleep.

Ted Rhodes virtually adopted Elder for three years, taking him into his home and teaching him all he could about the game of golf. In 1968, Elder was ready, financially and in experience, to join the PGA tour. In that first season, he tied with Jack Nicklaus and Frank Beard in the American Golf Classic at Akron, Ohio.

Television covered the play-off. Beard was eliminated at the first extra hole. Nicklaus sank 16- and 30-footers to hold off Elder's challenge and then, on the fourth of the sudden-death holes, Nicklaus made a birdie for outright victory. Elder had to be content with other satisfactions, not least the remark by PGA president Maxwell Stanford: 'Elder did more for Negro golf in forty-five minutes than everybody else had done in forty-five years.'

It was a pardonable overstatement, but there is no doubt that Elder's composure, and his sporting acceptance of those cruel thrusts from Nicklaus's putter, won him enormous personal popularity and respect. If Rhodes and Sifford had largely won the legalistic battle for integration in golf, Elder had won a considerable victory in the campaign for what liberals like to call the hearts and minds of men.

When Lee Elder walks out of the Augusta National club-house next April and steps up to the first tee, I am sure he will be given an enormous ovation. His appearance on that occasion, as I have said, will be purely symbolic in the struggle long since won but none the less welcome for that.

It was twenty-two years after Elder played in the 1975 Masters that Tiger Woods became the first black golfer to win a major championship when he won by 12 strokes at Augusta.

(OBSERVER 1974)

Turning to Turnberry

Ever since the Royal and Ancient Golf Club announced that the 1977 Open Championship was to be played at Turnberry, I have had a vision of a district nurse in an old Morris pulling onto the A77 near Maybole at about six in the morning after attending an all-night confinement.

It is the same nurse whose ill-judged manoeuvrings at Blairgowrie a few years ago contrived to hook all the press tent telephone cables onto her rear bumper and rip them from their moorings five minutes before edition time.

On this occasion, muggy from chloroform fumes and the even more potent vapours of the Glenlivet used to wet the baby's head, she fails to observe an approaching tanker. The tanker jack-knifes and overturns, completely blocking the road.

Four hours later, at Turnberry, the starter for the Open Championship is hoarse from calling in vain the names of competitors. Traffic by now is backed up solid all the way north to Stirling. Glasgow is paralysed. Not one golfer can get to the course. But wait, what's this? An unknown assistant who has slept in the car park steps forward as his name is called. He is the only competitor not disqualified and wins with scores of 79, 82, 91, 107, playing with a marker.

Despite reassurances from the local police, I cannot entirely erase that vision from my mind, and will confine conjecture about possible winners to players whom I know to be staying within easy walking distance of the first tee.

If golf were a game which invariably rewarded the best man,

there would be no problem. We could have the presentation ceremony first, hand the cup to Jack Nicklaus and then play four rounds to determine the runner-up. But you can never be sure. The last time I stayed at Turnberry, my bedroom window was torn out by the wind, and hailstones the size of golf balls tore horizontally across the room like cannonballs.

Nicklaus could get frostbite, or he might get hungry during a practice round and innocently expose himself to the Scottish outside catering industry. Not even Nicklaus can play golf with stomach cramp or coffee poisoning. Cold mutton pies have cost many a good man an Open. Or he might just go broody, the way he can at times.

We must consider other possibles. Hubert Green? On a Scottish links, yardages do not mean very much. You have to be able to judge a shot by eye and, frankly, Green's eyes are too close together to give accurate depth perception. Ask any optician, or maker of rangefinders. You need the optics well spaced for triangulation.

Tom Watson has most of the credentials, good current form and a satisfactory spread between the eyes. I am not sure that his driving is certain enough for Turnberry. The winner will have to be long and inordinately straight off the tee because the rough is the special tungsten grass peculiar to the district. I am told that the local sheep get through two or three sets of teeth a year.

Mention of sheep naturally raises the question of Tom Weiskopf. He has the game for Turnberry, but I fear the sight of distant flocks might distract him. You cannot concentrate on golf if you are itching to reach for a gun.

Ben Crenshaw? Now, there's a likely candidate. He has managed to convince himself that he likes links golf – and there's a neat psychological trick if you can pull it, rather like developing a taste for dining with the Borgias. My only reservation is that he has shown an unhealthy respect for the traditions of golf. He reads Bernard Darwin, and it would not surprise me to learn that he knows how to spell Auchterlonie and even pronounce it. I fear that playing in Scotland he may succumb to all that 'cradle of the game' rubbish and will therefore lack the essential contempt for bumble and bounce golf.

So far as I am aware, there is absolutely nothing wrong with Gary Player. The last time I saw him he had discovered the secret of golf, and of putting, and was at peace with the world. He therefore faces a crisis and, unless his fertile imagination can conjure up an insuperable barrier to overcome, he is a goner. There must be some challenge left for him to conquer. He might try an imaginary broken leg, for instance, have himself put in plaster from hip to ankle, and become the first man to win an Open on crutches. Well, it is just a suggestion, Gary.

Severiano Ballesteros has already used the bad-back ploy, in winning the Uniroyal, and I doubt if there is enough cortisone in the world to straighten out his driving sufficiently to tackle Turnberry. He is going to win the Open some time, but not this year.

Graham Marsh is also going to win the Open in due course, although at the moment he is so thoroughly over-golfed that I fear even his iron constitution and implacable will cannot guarantee four good rounds. In short, nobody is going to win the Open. Come Saturday evening, I believe that everyone will have lost the Open, except one. We shall acclaim him the winner but in truth he ought to be designated the non-loser.

As forecasts go, pretty good. Tom Watson won that Open by playing the final two rounds in 65–65. He birdied the last two holes and beat Jack Nicklaus by a shot after one of the greatest last days in Open history. Hubert Green was third, the only other player to finish below par but 11 shots behind Watson. Ben Crenshaw tied for fifth. Seve Ballesteros did win the Open two years later. But Graham Marsh never did win a major championship.

(Observer 1977)

Ryder Cup requiem

So the Ryder Cup is dead. It was quietly put down to prevent further suffering and the body was interred in an unmarked grave.

Even though the murderers – or enlightened humanitarians, according to your views on euthanasia – unscrewed the brass nameplate from the coffin and attached it to a new competition in the hope of persuading us that the Ryder Cup lives on in more vigorous form than ever, the fact is that the living spirit of this unique contest exists no more.

The reasons for killing the Ryder Cup were expressed in one of those famous American offers which are impossible to refuse: beef up your team with outsiders and give us a real match or we quit. As a result, next year's [1979] match will be between America and Europe, which may well prove to be a close and exciting encounter, but it will not be a Ryder Cup match.

Of course, the Ryder Cup match was helplessly, if not hopelessly, one-sided. One reason for this was the curious attitude of the British PGA, which has long since lost any interest in winning the trophy.

In America, the Ryder Cup rates somewhere between the Tennessee Frog Jumping Contest and the Alabama Melon Pip Spitting Championship, although the players themselves have always taken it seriously until Tom Weiskopf declined to play in favour of a week's holiday shooting sheep.

In Britain, the Ryder Cup match has always been a cause for national hysteria, born of the hope that one day David might fluke a lucky shot between the eyes of Goliath. That public obsession meant big money, and the PGA has seen the match almost solely as a golden opportunity to dip its bread in the gravy. Team selection was allowed to look after itself. Since defeat was inevitable, it did not really matter who the vanquished might be.

The team was chosen on a points basis, according to performance during the season. The side was, therefore, made up from the half-dozen obvious choices, the good players who could acquire the required number of points from a limited playing programme, and the balance came from among those golfers who slogged away week after week and thereby made the grade as much on good attendance as good golf.

The players themselves wanted it this way, because the system appeared to be fair, and there are considerable perks to be picked up from having a Ryder Cup badge on your blazer pocket, even though you may be an indifferent performer. The result was that never in my experience have I known a British and Irish Ryder Cup team made up from the best match players in these islands. The formula was to gather together the players who had made most money competing in a different game altogether.

No doubt a similar system will be used to nominate the players to represent Europe, with a few selective places to cover individual cases such as Peter Oosterhuis, who lives and competes in America. Whether this team will play with the same fire under the European banner as the Ryder Cup teams did, I take leave to doubt, just as I doubt whether the public interest (and with it the public income) will be as intense.

The theory is that since Spain has won the World Cup for the past two years it follows that Spanish players will be an asset to the enlarged Ryder Cup squad. This view overlooks the undoubted fact that one of the reasons behind Spain's magnificent successes was that Severiano Ballesteros, partnered first by Manuel Pinero and next by Tony Garrido, was playing for

Spain. Will they be inspired to rise to such heights by a spirit of European unity?

Likewise, patriotic feelings released in Brian Huggett such determination that he became transformed as a golfer to match the best that America could set against him. Will his successors find the same inspiration in a European team, partnered with men who cannot speak the same language and whose only bond is an envy of American prize rates?

We shall see in due course. I only wish they would provide a new trophy and a new name for this new competition.

In 1978, it was announced that henceforth the Great Britain & Ireland Ryder Cup team would be reinforced by the inclusion of continental golfers in the biennial match against the United States. This column proved to be a rare case of Dobereiner in fact getting it wrong, although no one was more delighted than him at the fervour with which continental golfers like Seve Balles-teros and Manuel Pinero, and Germany's Bernhard Langer, were fired up for the European cause every two years.

(OBSERVER 1978)

A European victory will save the Ryder Cup

From time to time I receive letters from *Golf Digest* readers who obviously believe me to be an American, working at the office in Connecticut. This is confession time. I must admit I am British, a mongrel comprising English, Welsh, German, Scottish, Blackfoot Indian, Danish and Canadian, plus a dash of monosodium glutamate, no doubt, but British.

I love America – it is my second home – and I have many American friends. But even though I try to be objective most of the time, every second year when the Ryder Cup comes around, I want us to win.

Since 1957, that has been like wanting some of my other wilder fantasies (such as a meaningful relationship with Marilyn Monroe, a million-dollar windfall and a single-figure handicap) to come true. I may be biased, but I have reasons to support my prejudice.

Take the course where this year's [1985] match is to be played. The Belfry, near Birmingham, England, is a long parkland course with excellent greens, historically just the place to favour the American power game and putting wizardry, the two elements that normally kill the British team.

However, significant changes have occurred to shift the balance of advantage. Most importantly, the British and Irish team has now expanded into the European team, and last year Mark McCormack's international ranking system made Severiano Ballesteros the best player in the world. Bernhard Langer of Germany was rated tenth and has since moved up the ladder through his victories in the Masters and the Heritage Classic.

Nick Faldo was ninth and Sandy Lyle of Scotland had the lowest stroke average in the world last year. Captain Tony Jacklin's wild-card choices will be match play specialists. His overriding criterion will be 'bottle', a word I shall not attempt to explain in a respectable magazine, save to say that it derives from the vulgar hinterland of London's East End, meaning courage or guts.

In the past, the British team has been the underdog, apprehensive at meeting the Americans (and rightly so). The British had inferiority complexes that had them beaten before they began. That changed last time (the Americans squeaked by $14\frac{1}{2}$–$13\frac{1}{2}$, and now the Europeans are confident of victory and relishing the prospect of battle.

Furthermore, American golf is in a trough. The giants who have dominated the game for generations are declining, and new stars have not yet risen to take their place. The team certainly will lack experience. It will fight like hell, because American teams always do and the American counterpunch is a byword in Ryder Cup history. But on balance, I believe there is a very good chance the strength of the opposition and the enormity of the occasion could be too much for them.

The occasion? That may seem a strange concept to Americans because in the United States the Ryder Cup is virtually played in private, ignored by most golfers and scarcely rating a mention in the papers. Why should it? After all, it is a formality, about as exciting as watching the rerun of a football game when you already know the result. The reverse is the case in Britain, where it rates alongside World War Three, for public hysteria.

And that brings me to my final point, which is that it would do international golf a power of good if the Europeans did win. In 1987, the match is to be played at Muirfield Village Golf Club, pride and joy of Jack Nicklaus. Nicklaus does not do things by halves. He started planning for the match a year ago, and he will turn it into a major production. He will generate public interest and get the networks eating out of his hand. But it would help him enormously if the Americans were pre-sented as avenging angels, out to restore the pride of American golf.

In short, a European victory could turn the Ryder Cup into a major international event that captures the imagination of two continents every other year. And we can all drink to that.

> ... *on the other hand, Peter was pretty spot-on this time. An inspired European team won the 1985 Ryder Cup match by $16\frac{1}{2}$ points to $11\frac{1}{2}$, the first time the United States had been defeated since 1957. Two years on, Europe inflicted the first defeat on American soil, by 15–13 at Muirfield Village. The Ryder Cup is now indeed golf's 'fifth major'.*

(GOLF DIGEST 1985)

SEVEN: END

The links of Pratts Bottom

One of Bernard Darwin's most memorable and best-loved essays is entitled 'The Links of Eiderdown'. He relieves the tedium of being confined to bed for the day by creating golf holes – classic linksland holes, of course, given the billowing nature of the site – simply by adjusting the position of his legs.

Fifty years later, and about four miles from Darwin's, on the southern aspect of a noble beech wood called Pratts Bottom, your ancient correspondent finds himself similarly reduced to a horizontal state.

Not having Darwin's talent or temperament for whipping up a literary soufflé, I arrange my ingredients rather differently. First, I introduce a variety of cushions and pillows. My *pièce de résistance* is a stout walking stick.

Vigorous belabouring with the cane enables me to produce instant 3D designs of 'ideal' golf holes. Better still, I can express my opinion of a hole with a viciously destructive attack and immediately take remedial action.

The most public-spirited application of my powers, as I so judged, was to save some of Britain's historic links by making them worthy tests for the Open Championship. Naturally, my thoughts turned first to Royal St George's. Among American professionals, opinions of Royal St George's are diametrically opposed.

One faction insists there are no points in creating a golf course until they have a golf *club*. I have a certain sympathy for this view after seeing Jack Nicklaus inquire as to the whereabouts of his locker for the Open and watching him being directed to the fifth peg along the back corridor.

But on this occasion, I had to go along with the faction that feels there is no point in creating a golf club until they had a valid golf course. Actually, St George's does not need all that much attention. It is just that when you get to a really fiendish hole like the fourth, and find yourself having to jump on a 2-iron into the prevailing wind to half a small green set hard against the out-of-bounds, you assume some lunacy is the norm. Far from it. A tickle here, a tweak there and you have a high proposition of quality.

The fourteenth hole, the Suez Canal, is a dreadful hole but with the potential to match a superb finish. The eighteenth could do with greater potential for drama than the odd streaker, but a few whacks with the cane could take care of both problems.

Turnberry is probably at greater risk of losing the Open. The good news is that this majestic seascape self-evidently conceals beneath its fescue dustcover the most magnificent links in the world.

This exciting prospect was quickly revealed by my flashing cane. It took just two mighty slashes to transform the nothingness of the notorious Bruce's Castle hole. Local lore has it that one lucky fellow once managed to hold his drive on the severest hog's-back fairway I have ever seen and one of the least-distinguished par 4s in championship golf. But a whack on the cushion tee slewed it through 45 degrees and produced the most dramatic par 3 in British golf, played over the foaming breakers to a green in front of the lighthouse.

By setting the next tee around the other side of the lighthouse, a white-knuckle par 5 is revealed that makes the eighth at Pebble Beach appear humdrum by comparison.

My next move was to identify and preserve Turnberry's classic holes, pitifully few of them, and then give full rein to my imagination. It might be felt that a multicourse development should share the natural goodies equally among the three courses. Anybody propounding such democratic nonsense would have felt the full weight of my cane across his flanks. I jealously appropriated every inch of coastline for the course of courses.

By the same token, can you justify pouring such resources into a course that can only truly come into its own once every five years or so? Indeed you can. I guarantee that one exposure on TV would put Turnberry right up there alongside St Andrews at the top of every golfer's 'must play' list.

The transformation is there for the making. I have the magic wand. Will travel.

This column, completed in summer 1996, was published post-humously in the October issue of Golf Digest. *As the magazine remarked in a footnote, even at the end, Peter 'was still at the top of his game'.*

(GOLF DIGEST 1996)